M Ometrix
EST PREPARATION

DSST®

ntroduction to Law nforcement xam Secrets tudy Guide

a registered trademark of Prometric LLC, which is not affiliated with Mometrix Test Preparation and does orse this product.

DEAR FUTURE EXAM SUCCESS STORY

First of all, **THANK YOU** for purchasing Mometrix study materials!

Second, congratulations! You are one of the few determined test-takers who are committed to doing whatever it takes to excel on your exam. **You have come to the right place.** We developed these study materials with one goal in mind: to deliver you the information you need in a format that's concise and easy to use.

In addition to optimizing your guide for the content of the test, we've outlined our recommended steps for breaking down the preparation process into small, attainable goals so you can make sure you stay on track.

We've also analyzed the entire test-taking process, identifying the most common pitfalls and showing how you can overcome them and be ready for any curveball the test throws you.

Standardized testing is one of the biggest obstacles on your road to success, which only increases the importance of doing well in the high-pressure, high-stakes environment of test day. Your results on this test could have a significant impact on your future, and this guide provides the information and practical advice to help you achieve your full potential on test day.

Your success is our success

We would love to hear from you! If you would like to share the story of your exam success or if you have any questions or comments in regard to our products, please contact us at **800-673-8175** or **support@mometrix.com**.

Thanks again for your business and we wish you continued success!

Sincerely,
The Mometrix Test Preparation Team

Need more help? Check out our flashcards at:
http://MometrixFlashcards.com/DSST

Written and edited by the Mometrix Exam Secrets Test Prep Team
Printed in the United States of America

Table of Contents

Introduction

Thank you for purchasing this resource! You have made the choice to prepare yourself for a test that could have a huge impact on your future, and this guide is designed to help you be fully ready for test day. Obviously, it's important to have a solid understanding of the test material, but you also need to be prepared for the unique environment and stressors of the test, so that you can perform to the best of your abilities.

For this purpose, the first section that appears in this guide is the **Secret Keys**. We've devoted countless hours to meticulously researching what works and what doesn't, and we've boiled down our findings to the five most impactful steps you can take to improve your performance on the test. We start at the beginning with study planning and move through the preparation process, all the way to the testing strategies that will help you get the most out of what you know when you're finally sitting in front of the test.

We recommend that you start preparing for your test as far in advance as possible. However, if you've bought this guide as a last-minute study resource and only have a few days before your test, we recommend that you skip over the first two Secret Keys since they address a long-term study plan.

If you struggle with **test anxiety**, we strongly encourage you to check out our recommendations for how you can overcome it. Test anxiety is a formidable foe, but it can be beaten, and we want to make sure you have the tools you need to defeat it.

Secret Key #1 – Plan Big, Study Small

There's a lot riding on your performance. If you want to ace this test, you're going to need to keep your skills sharp and the material fresh in your mind. You need a plan that lets you review everything you need to know while still fitting in your schedule. We'll break this strategy down into three categories.

Information Organization

Start with the information you already have: the official test outline. From this, you can make a complete list of all the concepts you need to cover before the test. Organize these concepts into groups that can be studied together, and create a list of any related vocabulary you need to learn so you can brush up on any difficult terms. You'll want to keep this vocabulary list handy once you actually start studying since you may need to add to it along the way.

Time Management

Once you have your set of study concepts, decide how to spread them out over the time you have left before the test. Break your study plan into small, clear goals so you have a manageable task for each day and know exactly what you're doing. Then just focus on one small step at a time. When you manage your time this way, you don't need to spend hours at a time studying. Studying a small block of content for a short period each day helps you retain information better and avoid stressing over how much you have left to do. You can relax knowing that you have a plan to cover everything in time. In order for this strategy to be effective though, you have to start studying early and stick to your schedule. Avoid the exhaustion and futility that comes from last-minute cramming!

Study Environment

The environment you study in has a big impact on your learning. Studying in a coffee shop, while probably more enjoyable, is not likely to be as fruitful as studying in a quiet room. It's important to keep distractions to a minimum. You're only planning to study for a short block of time, so make the most of it. Don't pause to check your phone or get up to find a snack. It's also important to **avoid multitasking**. Research has consistently shown that multitasking will make your studying dramatically less effective. Your study area should also be comfortable and well-lit so you don't have the distraction of straining your eyes or sitting on an uncomfortable chair.

The time of day you study is also important. You want to be rested and alert. Don't wait until just before bedtime. Study when you'll be most likely to comprehend and remember. Even better, if you know what time of day your test will be, set that time aside for study. That way your brain will be used to working on that subject at that specific time and you'll have a better chance of recalling information.

Finally, it can be helpful to team up with others who are studying for the same test. Your actual studying should be done in as isolated an environment as possible, but the work of organizing the information and setting up the study plan can be divided up. In between study sessions, you can discuss with your teammates the concepts that you're all studying and quiz each other on the details. Just be sure that your teammates are as serious about the test as you are. If you find that your study time is being replaced with social time, you might need to find a new team.

Secret Key #2 – Make Your Studying Count

You're devoting a lot of time and effort to preparing for this test, so you want to be absolutely certain it will pay off. This means doing more than just reading the content and hoping you can remember it on test day. It's important to make every minute of study count. There are two main areas you can focus on to make your studying count.

Retention

It doesn't matter how much time you study if you can't remember the material. You need to make sure you are retaining the concepts. To check your retention of the information you're learning, try recalling it at later times with minimal prompting. Try carrying around flashcards and glance at one or two from time to time or ask a friend who's also studying for the test to quiz you.

To enhance your retention, look for ways to put the information into practice so that you can apply it rather than simply recalling it. If you're using the information in practical ways, it will be much easier to remember. Similarly, it helps to solidify a concept in your mind if you're not only reading it to yourself but also explaining it to someone else. Ask a friend to let you teach them about a concept you're a little shaky on (or speak aloud to an imaginary audience if necessary). As you try to summarize, define, give examples, and answer your friend's questions, you'll understand the concepts better and they will stay with you longer. Finally, step back for a big picture view and ask yourself how each piece of information fits with the whole subject. When you link the different concepts together and see them working together as a whole, it's easier to remember the individual components.

Finally, practice showing your work on any multi-step problems, even if you're just studying. Writing out each step you take to solve a problem will help solidify the process in your mind, and you'll be more likely to remember it during the test.

Modality

Modality simply refers to the means or method by which you study. Choosing a study modality that fits your own individual learning style is crucial. No two people learn best in exactly the same way, so it's important to know your strengths and use them to your advantage.

For example, if you learn best by visualization, focus on visualizing a concept in your mind and draw an image or a diagram. Try color-coding your notes, illustrating them, or creating symbols that will trigger your mind to recall a learned concept. If you learn best by hearing or discussing information, find a study partner who learns the same way or read aloud to yourself. Think about how to put the information in your own words. Imagine that you are giving a lecture on the topic and record yourself so you can listen to it later.

For any learning style, flashcards can be helpful. Organize the information so you can take advantage of spare moments to review. Underline key words or phrases. Use different colors for different categories. Mnemonic devices (such as creating a short list in which every item starts with the same letter) can also help with retention. Find what works best for you and use it to store the information in your mind most effectively and easily.

Secret Key #3 – Practice the Right Way

Your success on test day depends not only on how many hours you put into preparing, but also on whether you prepared the right way. It's good to check along the way to see if your studying is paying off. One of the most effective ways to do this is by taking practice tests to evaluate your progress. Practice tests are useful because they show exactly where you need to improve. Every time you take a practice test, pay special attention to these three groups of questions:

- The questions you got wrong
- The questions you had to guess on, even if you guessed right
- The questions you found difficult or slow to work through

This will show you exactly what your weak areas are, and where you need to devote more study time. Ask yourself why each of these questions gave you trouble. Was it because you didn't understand the material? Was it because you didn't remember the vocabulary? Do you need more repetitions on this type of question to build speed and confidence? Dig into those questions and figure out how you can strengthen your weak areas as you go back to review the material.

Additionally, many practice tests have a section explaining the answer choices. It can be tempting to read the explanation and think that you now have a good understanding of the concept. However, an explanation likely only covers part of the question's broader context. Even if the explanation makes perfect sense, **go back and investigate** every concept related to the question until you're positive you have a thorough understanding.

As you go along, keep in mind that the practice test is just that: practice. Memorizing these questions and answers will not be very helpful on the actual test because it is unlikely to have any of the same exact questions. If you only know the right answers to the sample questions, you won't be prepared for the real thing. **Study the concepts** until you understand them fully, and then you'll be able to answer any question that shows up on the test.

It's important to wait on the practice tests until you're ready. If you take a test on your first day of study, you may be overwhelmed by the amount of material covered and how much you need to learn. Work up to it gradually.

On test day, you'll need to be prepared for answering questions, managing your time, and using the test-taking strategies you've learned. It's a lot to balance, like a mental marathon that will have a big impact on your future. Like training for a marathon, you'll need to start slowly and work your way up. When test day arrives, you'll be ready.

Start with the strategies you've read in the first two Secret Keys—plan your course and study in the way that works best for you. If you have time, consider using multiple study resources to get different approaches to the same concepts. It can be helpful to see difficult concepts from more than one angle. Then find a good source for practice tests. Many times, the test website will suggest potential study resources or provide sample tests.

Practice Test Strategy

If you're able to find at least three practice tests, we recommend this strategy:

Untimed and Open-Book Practice

Take the first test with no time constraints and with your notes and study guide handy. Take your time and focus on applying the strategies you've learned.

Timed and Open-Book Practice

Take the second practice test open-book as well, but set a timer and practice pacing yourself to finish in time.

Timed and Closed-Book Practice

Take any other practice tests as if it were test day. Set a timer and put away your study materials. Sit at a table or desk in a quiet room, imagine yourself at the testing center, and answer questions as quickly and accurately as possible.

Keep repeating timed and closed-book tests on a regular basis until you run out of practice tests or it's time for the actual test. Your mind will be ready for the schedule and stress of test day, and you'll be able to focus on recalling the material you've learned.

Secret Key #4 – Pace Yourself

Once you're fully prepared for the material on the test, your biggest challenge on test day will be managing your time. Just knowing that the clock is ticking can make you panic even if you have plenty of time left. Work on pacing yourself so you can build confidence against the time constraints of the exam. Pacing is a difficult skill to master, especially in a high-pressure environment, so **practice is vital**.

Set time expectations for your pace based on how much time is available. For example, if a section has 60 questions and the time limit is 30 minutes, you know you have to average 30 seconds or less per question in order to answer them all. Although 30 seconds is the hard limit, set 25 seconds per question as your goal, so you reserve extra time to spend on harder questions. When you budget extra time for the harder questions, you no longer have any reason to stress when those questions take longer to answer.

Don't let this time expectation distract you from working through the test at a calm, steady pace, but keep it in mind so you don't spend too much time on any one question. Recognize that taking extra time on one question you don't understand may keep you from answering two that you do understand later in the test. If your time limit for a question is up and you're still not sure of the answer, mark it and move on, and come back to it later if the time and the test format allow. If the testing format doesn't allow you to return to earlier questions, just make an educated guess; then put it out of your mind and move on.

On the easier questions, be careful not to rush. It may seem wise to hurry through them so you have more time for the challenging ones, but it's not worth missing one if you know the concept and just didn't take the time to read the question fully. Work efficiently but make sure you understand the question and have looked at all of the answer choices, since more than one may seem right at first.

Even if you're paying attention to the time, you may find yourself a little behind at some point. You should speed up to get back on track, but do so wisely. Don't panic; just take a few seconds less on each question until you're caught up. Don't guess without thinking, but do look through the answer choices and eliminate any you know are wrong. If you can get down to two choices, it is often worthwhile to guess from those. Once you've chosen an answer, move on and don't dwell on any that you skipped or had to hurry through. If a question was taking too long, chances are it was one of the harder ones, so you weren't as likely to get it right anyway.

On the other hand, if you find yourself getting ahead of schedule, it may be beneficial to slow down a little. The more quickly you work, the more likely you are to make a careless mistake that will affect your score. You've budgeted time for each question, so don't be afraid to spend that time. Practice an efficient but careful pace to get the most out of the time you have.

Secret Key #5 – Have a Plan for Guessing

When you're taking the test, you may find yourself stuck on a question. Some of the answer choices seem better than others, but you don't see the one answer choice that is obviously correct. What do you do?

The scenario described above is very common, yet most test takers have not effectively prepared for it. Developing and practicing a plan for guessing may be one of the single most effective uses of your time as you get ready for the exam.

In developing your plan for guessing, there are three questions to address:

- When should you start the guessing process?
- How should you narrow down the choices?
- Which answer should you choose?

When to Start the Guessing Process

Unless your plan for guessing is to select C every time (which, despite its merits, is not what we recommend), you need to leave yourself enough time to apply your answer elimination strategies. Since you have a limited amount of time for each question, that means that if you're going to give yourself the best shot at guessing correctly, you have to decide quickly whether or not you will guess.

Of course, the best-case scenario is that you don't have to guess at all, so first, see if you can answer the question based on your knowledge of the subject and basic reasoning skills. Focus on the key words in the question and try to jog your memory of related topics. Give yourself a chance to bring the knowledge to mind, but once you realize that you don't have (or you can't access) the knowledge you need to answer the question, it's time to start the guessing process.

It's almost always better to start the guessing process too early than too late. It only takes a few seconds to remember something and answer the question from knowledge. Carefully eliminating wrong answer choices takes longer. Plus, going through the process of eliminating answer choices can actually help jog your memory.

Summary: Start the guessing process as soon as you decide that you can't answer the question based on your knowledge.

How to Narrow Down the Choices

The next chapter in this book (**Test-Taking Strategies**) includes a wide range of strategies for how to approach questions and how to look for answer choices to eliminate. You will definitely want to read those carefully, practice them, and figure out which ones work best for you. Here though, we're going to address a mindset rather than a particular strategy.

Your odds of guessing an answer correctly depend on how many options you are choosing from.

Number of options left	5	4	3	2	1
Odds of guessing correctly	20%	25%	33%	50%	100%

You can see from this chart just how valuable it is to be able to eliminate incorrect answers and make an educated guess, but there are two things that many test takers do that cause them to miss out on the benefits of guessing:

- Accidentally eliminating the correct answer
- Selecting an answer based on an impression

We'll look at the first one here, and the second one in the next section.

To avoid accidentally eliminating the correct answer, we recommend a thought exercise called **the $5 challenge**. In this challenge, you only eliminate an answer choice from contention if you are willing to bet $5 on it being wrong. Why $5? Five dollars is a small but not insignificant amount of money. It's an amount you could afford to lose but wouldn't want to throw away. And while losing $5 once might not hurt too much, doing it twenty times will set you back $100. In the same way, each small decision you make—eliminating a choice here, guessing on a question there—won't by itself impact your score very much, but when you put them all together, they can make a big difference. By holding each answer choice elimination decision to a higher standard, you can reduce the risk of accidentally eliminating the correct answer.

The $5 challenge can also be applied in a positive sense: If you are willing to bet $5 that an answer choice *is* correct, go ahead and mark it as correct.

Summary: Only eliminate an answer choice if you are willing to bet $5 that it is wrong.

Which Answer to Choose

You're taking the test. You've run into a hard question and decided you'll have to guess. You've eliminated all the answer choices you're willing to bet $5 on. Now you have to pick an answer. Why do we even need to talk about this? Why can't you just pick whichever one you feel like when the time comes?

The answer to these questions is that if you don't come into the test with a plan, you'll rely on your impression to select an answer choice, and if you do that, you risk falling into a trap. The test writers know that everyone who takes their test will be guessing on some of the questions, so they intentionally write wrong answer choices to seem plausible. You still have to pick an answer though, and if the wrong answer choices are designed to look right, how can you ever be sure that you're not falling for their trap? The best solution we've found to this dilemma is to take the decision out of your hands entirely. Here is the process we recommend:

Once you've eliminated any choices that you are confident (willing to bet $5) are wrong, select the first remaining choice as your answer.

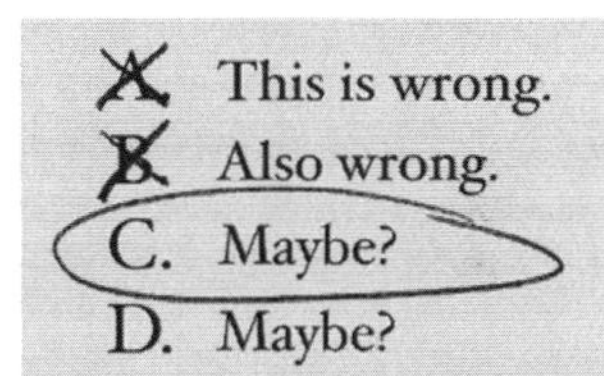

Whether you choose to select the first remaining choice, the second, or the last, the important thing is that you use some preselected standard. Using this approach guarantees that you will not be enticed into selecting an answer choice that looks right, because you are not basing your decision on how the answer choices look.

This is not meant to make you question your knowledge. Instead, it is to help you recognize the difference between your knowledge and your impressions. There's a huge difference between thinking an answer is right because of what you know, and thinking an answer is right because it looks or sounds like it should be right.

Summary: To ensure that your selection is appropriately random, make a predetermined selection from among all answer choices you have not eliminated.

Test-Taking Strategies

This section contains a list of test-taking strategies that you may find helpful as you work through the test. By taking what you know and applying logical thought, you can maximize your chances of answering any question correctly!

It is very important to realize that every question is different and every person is different: no single strategy will work on every question, and no single strategy will work for every person. That's why we've included all of them here, so you can try them out and determine which ones work best for different types of questions and which ones work best for you.

Question Strategies

☑ Read Carefully

Read the question and the answer choices carefully. Don't miss the question because you misread the terms. You have plenty of time to read each question thoroughly and make sure you understand what is being asked. Yet a happy medium must be attained, so don't waste too much time. You must read carefully and efficiently.

☑ Contextual Clues

Look for contextual clues. If the question includes a word you are not familiar with, look at the immediate context for some indication of what the word might mean. Contextual clues can often give you all the information you need to decipher the meaning of an unfamiliar word. Even if you can't determine the meaning, you may be able to narrow down the possibilities enough to make a solid guess at the answer to the question.

☑ Prefixes

If you're having trouble with a word in the question or answer choices, try dissecting it. Take advantage of every clue that the word might include. Prefixes can be a huge help. Usually, they allow you to determine a basic meaning. *Pre-* means before, *post-* means after, *pro-* is positive, *de-* is negative. From prefixes, you can get an idea of the general meaning of the word and try to put it into context.

☑ Hedge Words

Watch out for critical hedge words, such as *likely, may, can, often, almost, mostly, usually, generally, rarely,* and *sometimes.* Question writers insert these hedge phrases to cover every possibility. Often an answer choice will be wrong simply because it leaves no room for exception. Be on guard for answer choices that have definitive words such as *exactly* and *always.*

☑ Switchback Words

Stay alert for *switchbacks.* These are the words and phrases frequently used to alert you to shifts in thought. The most common switchback words are *but, although,* and *however.* Others include *nevertheless, on the other hand, even though, while, in spite of, despite,* and *regardless of.* Switchback words are important to catch because they can change the direction of the question or an answer choice.

✅ Face Value

When in doubt, use common sense. Accept the situation in the problem at face value. Don't read too much into it. These problems will not require you to make wild assumptions. If you have to go beyond creativity and warp time or space in order to have an answer choice fit the question, then you should move on and consider the other answer choices. These are normal problems rooted in reality. The applicable relationship or explanation may not be readily apparent, but it is there for you to figure out. Use your common sense to interpret anything that isn't clear.

Answer Choice Strategies

✅ Answer Selection

The most thorough way to pick an answer choice is to identify and eliminate wrong answers until only one is left, then confirm it is the correct answer. Sometimes an answer choice may immediately seem right, but be careful. The test writers will usually put more than one reasonable answer choice on each question, so take a second to read all of them and make sure that the other choices are not equally obvious. As long as you have time left, it is better to read every answer choice than to pick the first one that looks right without checking the others.

✅ Answer Choice Families

An answer choice family consists of two (in rare cases, three) answer choices that are very similar in construction and cannot all be true at the same time. If you see two answer choices that are direct opposites or parallels, one of them is usually the correct answer. For instance, if one answer choice says that quantity *x* increases and another either says that quantity *x* decreases (opposite) or says that quantity *y* increases (parallel), then those answer choices would fall into the same family. An answer choice that doesn't match the construction of the answer choice family is more likely to be incorrect. Most questions will not have answer choice families, but when they do appear, you should be prepared to recognize them.

✅ Eliminate Answers

Eliminate answer choices as soon as you realize they are wrong, but make sure you consider all possibilities. If you are eliminating answer choices and realize that the last one you are left with is also wrong, don't panic. Start over and consider each choice again. There may be something you missed the first time that you will realize on the second pass.

✅ Avoid Fact Traps

Don't be distracted by an answer choice that is factually true but doesn't answer the question. You are looking for the choice that answers the question. Stay focused on what the question is asking for so you don't accidentally pick an answer that is true but incorrect. Always go back to the question and make sure the answer choice you've selected actually answers the question and is not merely a true statement.

✅ Extreme Statements

In general, you should avoid answers that put forth extreme actions as standard practice or proclaim controversial ideas as established fact. An answer choice that states the "process should be used in certain situations, if..." is much more likely to be correct than one that states the "process should be discontinued completely." The first is a calm rational statement and doesn't even make a definitive, uncompromising stance, using a hedge word *if* to provide wiggle room, whereas the second choice is far more extreme.

☑ BENCHMARK

As you read through the answer choices and you come across one that seems to answer the question well, mentally select that answer choice. This is not your final answer, but it's the one that will help you evaluate the other answer choices. The one that you selected is your benchmark or standard for judging each of the other answer choices. Every other answer choice must be compared to your benchmark. That choice is correct until proven otherwise by another answer choice beating it. If you find a better answer, then that one becomes your new benchmark. Once you've decided that no other choice answers the question as well as your benchmark, you have your final answer.

☑ PREDICT THE ANSWER

Before you even start looking at the answer choices, it is often best to try to predict the answer. When you come up with the answer on your own, it is easier to avoid distractions and traps because you will know exactly what to look for. The right answer choice is unlikely to be word-for-word what you came up with, but it should be a close match. Even if you are confident that you have the right answer, you should still take the time to read each option before moving on.

General Strategies

☑ TOUGH QUESTIONS

If you are stumped on a problem or it appears too hard or too difficult, don't waste time. Move on! Remember though, if you can quickly check for obviously incorrect answer choices, your chances of guessing correctly are greatly improved. Before you completely give up, at least try to knock out a couple of possible answers. Eliminate what you can and then guess at the remaining answer choices before moving on.

☑ CHECK YOUR WORK

Since you will probably not know every term listed and the answer to every question, it is important that you get credit for the ones that you do know. Don't miss any questions through careless mistakes. If at all possible, try to take a second to look back over your answer selection and make sure you've selected the correct answer choice and haven't made a costly careless mistake (such as marking an answer choice that you didn't mean to mark). This quick double check should more than pay for itself in caught mistakes for the time it costs.

☑ PACE YOURSELF

It's easy to be overwhelmed when you're looking at a page full of questions; your mind is confused and full of random thoughts, and the clock is ticking down faster than you would like. Calm down and maintain the pace that you have set for yourself. Especially as you get down to the last few minutes of the test, don't let the small numbers on the clock make you panic. As long as you are on track by monitoring your pace, you are guaranteed to have time for each question.

☑ DON'T RUSH

It is very easy to make errors when you are in a hurry. Maintaining a fast pace in answering questions is pointless if it makes you miss questions that you would have gotten right otherwise. Test writers like to include distracting information and wrong answers that seem right. Taking a little extra time to avoid careless mistakes can make all the difference in your test score. Find a pace that allows you to be confident in the answers that you select.

⊘ KEEP MOVING

Panicking will not help you pass the test, so do your best to stay calm and keep moving. Taking deep breaths and going through the answer elimination steps you practiced can help to break through a stress barrier and keep your pace.

Final Notes

The combination of a solid foundation of content knowledge and the confidence that comes from practicing your plan for applying that knowledge is the key to maximizing your performance on test day. As your foundation of content knowledge is built up and strengthened, you'll find that the strategies included in this chapter become more and more effective in helping you quickly sift through the distractions and traps of the test to isolate the correct answer.

Now that you're preparing to move forward into the test content chapters of this book, be sure to keep your goal in mind. As you read, think about how you will be able to apply this information on the test. If you've already seen sample questions for the test and you have an idea of the question format and style, try to come up with questions of your own that you can answer based on what you're reading. This will give you valuable practice applying your knowledge in the same ways you can expect to on test day.

Good luck and good studying!

History and Professional Movement of Law Enforcement

Code of Hammurabi and the Laws of Lipit-Ishtar

The Code of Hammurabi and the Laws of Lipit-Ishtar are some of the earliest codes of law known to man. The Code of Hammurabi was developed by the King of Babylon around 1750 b.c., while the Laws of Lipit-Ishtar were developed about 300 years earlier. Many of these laws dealt with basic ideas of justice—for example, how much a man would need to be paid if his ox were destroyed or what would happen if a theft took place. The full details of what these Codes contained is not available, but the basic importance is that they were early rules of law that set forth some of the basic principles of justice and fairness that still apply today.

First Modern Police Department

The first modern police department was created in London in 1829. Generally credited with this creation are Henry Fielding, Sir Robert Peel, and Patrick Colquhoun. Many of the citizens of England at this time were actually opposed to the creation of the police department because the British believed strongly in both personal liberties and local governments, and the idea of the police department seemed to run contrary to these ideals. Despite these objections, the police department was created. Many of the objections were dispensed with by the rules of police work being more clearly defined to be concerned with arresting offenders and doing detective work to solve crimes.

Influence of English Policing

The English heritage contributed the concepts of limited authority, local control, and the decentralized and fragmented police system. These principles were based on the ideals in London of local government and personal liberties and rights. The police did not have broad authority over all issues but instead had the right to do carefully defined duties, such as investigating specific crimes and working to apprehend those who broke the law. Further, there was not one centralized national police force, but different sects or branches of police stations available. These conditions exist in US police forces today throughout the country, where police work is carried out by precincts.

First Police Force in England

The first police force in England was the London Metropolitan Police Force. The first police force was created as part of a project by Robert Peel, who became the Home Secretary of London in 1822 and passed the Metropolitan Police Act in 1829 to establish the first police force. Before Peel was able to get the police force passed, he had to convince the House of Commons to overlook the objections of the English citizenry. Once Peel was successful and the Metropolitan Police Act went into effect, the first patrol from the Metropolitan Police Force went on the street on September 29, 1829.

Robert Peel

Robert Peel (1788–1850) is widely viewed as the father of modern policing because he was instrumental in the creation of the first Metropolitan Police Force in London. He served many functions in the British government, including secretary of state and prime minister. He was a conservative statesman and it was when he was serving as secretary of state that he convinced the House of Commons to pass the Metropolitan Police Act, despite some objections from the citizens living in London at the time. Because of the success of the first police force, based at Scotland Yard, by 1857, all of the cities within the United Kingdom were mandated to create their own police forces in the tradition of Peel.

1780 Gordon Riots

The 1780 Gordon Riots, a clash between Irish immigrants and English citizens was the event that led to the conclusion that London required a police force. The Gordon Riots were led by Catholics who did not want the passage of the Papists Act of 1778. The 1778 act was, ironically, an attempt to end discrimination against the Catholics that had been put into place in earlier acts, but Catholics were concerned that the passage of the Papists act would create more anti-Catholic sentiment than if the (rarely enforced) discriminatory rules were just left on the books. During the Gordon Riots, 40,000 to 60,000 people marched on the House of Parliament, and more people joined the riots as they were ongoing. Because of the lack of organization among the authorities and the lack of a proper police force, the authorities were not able to stop the riot from becoming a violent affair.

Henry Fielding

Henry Fielding (1707–1754) was responsible for primarily two contributions to the system of modern policing. First, he was an advocate of change and social awareness of the criminal issues plaguing London in the mid-1700s, condemning the unfair practice of killing citizens for petty crimes. Second, he, with his half-brother, organized a group of paid constables known as the Bow Street Runners, an organization that preceded the modern police force. He, along with Peel and Colquhoun, are widely viewed as being responsible for the creation of the idea of the modern police force. Fielding was a magistrate at the time the first police force was founded.

Patrick Colquhoun

Patrick Colquhoun was a magistrate credited with founding the Thames River Police. The force was designed to minimize and prevent the theft of the nearly 500,000 pounds of merchandise stolen each year from the cargo pool on the Thames called the Pool of London. Colquhoun started the force with 50 men, and the force was a great success, saving 122,000 pounds in the first year alone. Colquhoun wrote about the ideas that he had in the *Treatise on the Police of the Metropolis.* In his work, he advocated a structured police force in spite of criticism of the idea at the time.

Crime prevention

While earlier systems focused on punishing those who committed crimes, Robert Peel's new structure focused on deterrence through a pattern of preventive patrol. Police officers would have fixed "beats" in which they would be responsible for maintaining peace and order. The new focus on avoiding crime and preventing it instead of simply reacting to it made the London police force more successful than any prior policing organization at deterring crime. This idea of police having a regular beat is still used among police forces throughout the world today, and one of the primary goals of the police is prevention rather than reaction. Thus, this early idea has become accepted practice.

Early influences on American police forces

American policing also draws from Spanish and French law customs. In particular, the early French police force, called the Sureté, provided the inspiration for the FBI. The Sureté was a special, separate branch of the police force that was created to deal with the fact that the standard police force could not control or stop all crimes. The purpose of the Sureté was to work undercover in order to stop crime from the inside out, and it was so successful that after the creation of a 30-person Sureté, the crime rate was reduced by as much as 40 percent within the city of Paris by 1820. Today, American police officials both work undercover and use reformed criminals as informants to help them fight crime—both practices started by the Sureté.

First US Law Enforcement Officers

Initially, constables were among the first law enforcement officials in the US, along with "watchmen." These constables or watchmen performed the primary role of enforcing law and order prior to the colonial period in the 17th century. The early constables, however, weren't paid for their services—nor did they have an official uniform. Instead, they were simply elected at the local level and were generally paid if they were able to execute a warrant. The court that had issued the warrant made the payment to these early constables. After the 17th century, the role of constable shifted. Today, some constables serve warrants and subpoenas only, while in other states, constables are considered regular law enforcement officials.

Early US Police Departments

Many early police departments were established in the northeast due to the number of night watches in Plymouth and Boston in the 1630s and New York in the 1650s. A night watch was started in Philadelphia in 1700, and by 1808, St. Louis had established a Constabulary. The first day watch was created in Philadelphia in 1833. The early police forces became essential as cities grew and society became less and less rural. As a result of a larger population in a smaller area, crime such as public disturbances and riots began to grow and it became clear that there had to be a police force to control the problems. Still, many early Americans were resistant to the idea of creating a police force because of concern for civil liberties. In addition, many of those who acted as early police officials or watchmen were unpaid for their services.

Quality of Early Colonial Law Enforcement

Early law enforcement in the colonial United States was inefficient, lazy, and with little capacity to actually prevent crime. The agencies were reactive, not proactive, which meant that instead of trying stop crime before it happened or trying to deter crime, they simply reacted when a crime was reported and arrested and dealt with offenders then. Investigative methods were primitive and there wasn't necessarily widespread support for the idea of police forces and police investigation in most places. There were also too few watchmen for these early forces to be especially effective. Patronage meant favoritism and corruption.

Modern US Police Forces

Modern police forces began to be established in the US in the 1830s and 1840s. The specific time periods when police forces were established vary depending on the city and on the need for law enforcement officials. Examples include the Texas Rangers, who were formed in 1835, as well as the Boston and Philadelphia police departments, which were both formed in 1845. Many of the modern police forces that were formed were designed to deal with specific problems, such as rising urban crime as the US became less rural. For example, some early police forces were specifically designed to deal with the crimes committed by "outlaw Indians."

Texas Rangers

The Texas Rangers were the first established "state police" force. The Texas Rangers began in Austin, Texas, but had jurisdiction in the entire state of Texas. The creation of the Texas Rangers is often attributed to Stephen F. Austin, although this is unofficial. Many believe Stephen F. Austin was responsible for the creation because he wrote a call to arms in 1823 that prompted the creation of the Rangers 12 years later (in 1835). The Texas Rangers had a part in many of the major criminal cases of the early days, including the hunt for Bonnie and Clyde.

19TH CENTURY LAW ENFORCEMENT

Law enforcement in the 19th century is generally regarded as tumultuous. Violence was common—even violence of police officers against citizens—and police forces lacked professionalism entirely. Corruption and favoritism were rampant during the early 19th century, making enforcement of laws and deterrence of crime even more uncertain among those who curried favor with the police forces of the time. Still, as there was more attention given to the importance of private property, law enforcement officials did become somewhat more effective than the very earliest police officials (the constables and watchmen), who were largely unpaid, reactive, and ineffective at controlling crime.

AUGUST VOLLMER

August Vollmer, who was responsible for many of the lasting reforms that continue to influence American policing, is considered to be the father of criminal justice in America. Vollmer himself was involved in law enforcement, and became known as a legendary heroic figure after he stopped a train collision in downtown Berkeley, California. Because of his heroism, he was elected the town marshal in 1905 and then reelected in 1907. When the city of Berkeley created the role of chief of police in 1909, Vollmer was also elected to the post. After his election, he made significant changes in the police force, based in part on his military background and on studies he did of criminal psychology. Reforms he made based on his research include the creation of centralized police records and a standardized system of criminal investigation.

PROFESSIONALISM MOVEMENT

The movement that aimed to redefine and clean up the corruption in policing was referred to as the professionalism movement. The professionalism movement was pioneered largely by August Vollmer after he was appointed the chief of police in Berkeley, California. His purpose was to attempt to make police officers more professional and to help to streamline the way police departments functioned in order to increase professionalism. Efforts to that end included more screening of recruits and increased training programs. The training he provided to officers included both scientific principles to be used in the investigation of crimes and courses on police administration.

ALICE STEBBINS WELLS

Alice Stebbins Wells was the first female police officer born in the United States. She was hired by the Los Angeles police force in 1910 after she had petitioned the Los Angeles city council, the major, and the police chief. Wells became the leader of the policewoman movement that led to departments employing female police officers all across the country beginning in the 1910s. She wished to work in law enforcement to help protect the rights of women and children and she eventually founded the International association of Police Women. She traveled throughout America to help encourage the promotion of female police officers until her retirement in 1940.

BOSTON POLICE STRIKE

The Boston Police Strike began in September 1919 as a result of both poor working conditions as well as low wages. The police union was unable to form an agreement with then Police Commissioner Edwin Upton Curtis. Curtis not only refused to improve working conditions or pay a higher wage, but he also was opposed to the idea of any sort of police union at all. The strike led to a backlash against police unions, in part because of the minor crime sprees that occurred during Boston at the time of the strike, although the actual damage from these crime waves was minimal at best. American Federation of Labor leader Samuel Gompers eventually encouraged the police to return to work because he recognized that the strike was causing public sentiment to turn on police unions.

Police Racism

Police racism is a widespread problem wherein police engage in behaviors that are discriminatory toward minorities. Police racism can include racial profiling, where individuals of a certain race are targeted for abusive police behavior such as excessive searches or searches without a probable cause. Police racism was widespread in some areas during the early days of police forces and the primary targets tended to be African Americans. The problem of police racism did not begin to receive attention or attempts at reform until the Civil Rights movement of the 1960s, when issues of minority oppression and the lack of equality came to the forefront.

FBI and State Police Agencies

The Federal Bureau of Investigation and state police agencies were two new types of law enforcement agency that appeared in the years leading up to the First World War. The FBI was created under the authority of Title 28 in the US Code, which grants the US attorney general the right to appoint officials to identify and investigate crimes committed against the United States. The purpose of the FBI was to enforce federal laws, as well as to act as a centralized intelligence agency. The need for a federal agency like the FBI became very important in 1886, when the case of *Washbush, St. Louis & Pacific Railway Company vs. Illinois* was decided, in which the Supreme Court mandated that the individual states did not have the authority to regulate commerce between the states. This, then, became the job of the federal government.

The FBI was established by President Theodore Roosevelt as the Bureau of Investigation in 1908 to provide the federal government a full-time investigation agency. The purpose of the FBI was to govern federal laws regulating interstate commerce and other issues that the individual states were not able to regulate with their own state laws. The authority was found in Title 28 of the United States Code, which that granted the federal government the right to create officials to investigate crimes committed against the United States. At its inception, the FBI acted as both an investigating agency and a centralized intelligence agency.

First Modern State Police Organization

The Pennsylvania State Police (Constabulary) was the first modern state police organization. It was created on May 2, 1905 by the Pennsylvania General Assembly to deal with labor problems and unrest in Pennsylvania at the time. Governor Samuel Pennypacker then signed it into law. Incidents such as the Anthracite Coal Strike in 1902, the division between the coal miners and factory workers, and the high crime rates in Pennsylvania at the time led to the creation of this state police organization, which functioned similarly to the military—its officers were called troopers and they lived in barracks and were highly centralized. However, they did not establish an official training academy until years later, in 1924.

Crime Prevention and Investigation

Throughout the 1920s, police began to develop new techniques for investigating crimes and preventing them. Prior to the 20s, much of police work had been based on reacting when crimes were reported or observed, as opposed to actually taking steps toward crime prevention or investigating crimes that had already occurred. Changes had slowly begun to be made as police records become more centralized, police work became more professional, corruption was cut down, and the police began to develop techniques and patterns of investigation. By 1920, police were more focused on law enforcement as a total package, including identifying and tracking down those who had committed crimes of the recent past and crimes that were unsolved. This focus continues to this day.

Volstead Act

Law enforcement changed fundamentally due to the Volstead Act, which prohibited alcohol use or purchase. The police had to enforce this highly unpopular law, sometimes at the cost of the respect of citizens. This led to widespread anti-police sentiment. It also forced the police to be more proactive. However, the Volstead Act was impossible to enforce by either the Prohibitions Bureau or by the police in states that were cooperating with the enforcement requirements of the Volstead act. In fact, federal prisons, state prisons, and county jails became so overcrowded that those who were convicted of violations were offered "bargain days" in some states, where they were able to receive lighter sentences.

Effect of the Depression on View of Criminals

The stock market crash of 1929 led to the Depression of the 1930s, during which there were very few jobs available. There were runs on banks, as depositors tried to get their money out for fear of a bank collapse. Reform efforts, such as the New Deal, attempted to solve the problem, but many of those in society still struggled. Because of the distaste for a government that had created the situation of the Depression and that wasn't solving it, and because of the climate of despair and shortage, criminals like Bonnie and Clyde and John Dillinger began to be seen as almost heroic anti-authority or Robin Hood figures.

O.W. Wilson

Wilson was the superintendent of the Chicago Police Department, as well as the chief of police in Wichita, Kansas and Fullerton, California. Wilson was also responsible for writing *Police Administration,* a text that championed centralization and quickly became a seminal work for police administrators. He called for imposition of new standards of professionalism on police forces, led reform efforts aimed at corruption, and helped to pioneer new innovations that changed the shape of the police force and police work, such as a mobile crime laboratory and the concept of patrol cars. He also developed a formula for assigning patrol officers using mobile radios and two-way radios.

Technology

Technology has allowed for quicker communication; better record systems; the use of fingerprinting, toxicology, and enhanced evidence collection; and many other innovations that continue to influence police departments. Mobile crime labs allow for better collection and preservation of blood and other evidence at the scenes of crimes and have increased the importance of forensics. Centralized record keeping and fingerprint systems allow for police to keep better track of potential suspects and criminals and allow for the sharing of records between police departments. Even radios changed the way police work is done, allowing police officers to be able to get to crime scenes much more quickly and to be more efficient in dispatching instructions and information necessary in an emergency situation.

Public and Community Relations

In the 1960s, the anti–Vietnam War and Civil Rights movements caused police organizations to focus more closely on the rights of citizens. During the time of the antiwar movement, the shooting and killing of four protestors at Kent State University by the Ohio National Guard had shocked the sensitivities of the public. It created a widespread anti-authority sentiment that stretched to police forces throughout the country. Because of this, as well as civil rights efforts and a focus on police racism, police had to become more sensitive to community relations in order to remain effective and respected by the public.

J. Edgar Hoover

J. Edgar Hoover was responsible for the development of the 10 Most Wanted List, the Uniform Crime Reports, and the Crime Lab of the Federal Bureau of Investigation. The FBI 10 Most Wanted list is updated as fugitives are captured and is meant to reflect the prevailing, current state of affairs. There is generally a reward offered for anyone turning in information leading to the capture of one of the 10 most wanted individuals on the list. The aim is to encourage catching criminals who have eluded authorities. The Crime Lab, on the other hand, is aimed primarily at investigating and solving crimes. The UCR is a compilation of crime statistics across the United States.

Citizen Oversight

Citizen oversight is the idea that the input of the public is an important mechanism for police accountability. The citizen oversight movement began in the 1970s in approximately 80 percent of the 50 largest cities in the United States. The purpose of citizen oversight is to provide additional mechanisms to track police misconduct and bias and to make sure that any unfair or abusive police behavior is reported and stopped. The need for citizen oversight exists because often internal controls are ineffective at eliminating police abuses or corruption, since the police would not report other officers or provide a deterrent to officers against improper behavior.

Community Policing

Community policing is the philosophy that police departments should develop working relationships with neighborhood residents and that police should depend upon the citizenry to help fight crime and reduce fear by concentrating on quality-of-life issues. Community policing encourages partnerships between the police and the citizens of a community, such as organized neighborhood watch programs. The purpose is not only to help reduce crime by taking advantage of the help of those in the community, but also to assist in making sure that there is a good relationship between the police and the community and to increase the trust of community members in law enforcement officials.

Racial Profiling

Racial profiling is police use of race, appearance, or ethnicity in determining how to engage in law enforcement. For example, racial profiling may include pulling over a person who is driving simply because he is of a minority group and not because he has done anything wrong. Much attention has been paid to racial profiling and racial bias in law enforcement, and the official position is that racial profiling is not an appropriate course of action. Unfortunately, the phenomenon still exists despite efforts to provide more sensitivity training, education, and minority acceptance.

COP Services

Community-oriented policing (COP) grew under Bill Clinton, who called for police officers and police organizations to take a more proactive role in engaging American communities. COP involves police forces working together and forming partnerships with communities and individuals in attempts to encourage residents to help to make their own communities safe. Neighborhood watch programs are one such example of community policing. The other purpose of COP services and programs is to help encourage trust in the police force among members of the community as a whole. The hope is that by working together, both the community and the police will benefit and there will be more ways to deter crime and to deter criminals from behaving illegally.

Overview of the Criminal Justice System

Criminal Justice System

The three primary components of the criminal justice system in the United States are police, courts, and corrections. The purpose of the police is to deter crimes by taking an active role such as patrolling, investigating crimes, and gathering evidence. The purpose of the court system is to ensure that justice is done. Courts not only try criminals to ensure that only the guilty are put in jail, but they also help to enforce civil rights by throwing out evidence when constitutional violations took place by members of the police force or law enforcement during the investigation phase. Finally, the purpose of the corrections system is to rehabilitate and imprison those who have been found guilty of a crime.

Federal Court System

The federal court system is a three-tiered structure comprising the US district courts, the US court of appeals, and the US Supreme Court. US district courts hear cases arising out of federal law or the Constitution. Appellate courts hear cases whose resolution in district court is being disputed by one of the parties thereto. Every party has the opportunity to appeal the case at least once (with the exception of prosecutors, who are not allowed to retry an accused criminal who has been found innocent). The Supreme Court is the highest court, and once it makes a decision, all other courts are bound by it; no one has the right of appeal. The Supreme Court chooses which cases it hears.

State Court Systems

Most state court systems have three courts: trial, appellate, and the state supreme court. In some states, such as New York, the names are different, and the Supreme Court is actually the lowest court in the land and the first court where cases are heard. Much like in the federal system, trial courts hear the cases first. Appellate courts hear cases whose resolutions at trial are disputed, e.g., to make sure the trial court followed the law appropriately. The state supreme court hears cases appealed from the appellate court. As in the federal system, the state supreme courts are the highest courts of most states and generally do not have to take a case unless they choose to.

Supreme Court

Justices

There are nine justices on the Supreme Court, one of whom is the chief justice. Unlike most judges of lower courts, justices on the Supreme Court are not elected by the people. Instead, they are appointed by the President of the United States who is in office when a justice leaves the court. The reason justices are not elected is because it is believed that they would be more impartial if they were not subject to meeting the whims of the electorate. A Supreme Court justice is appointed for life and cannot be removed or resign. The purpose of lifetime appointments is also to make sure that justices are impartial.

Location

The Supreme Court is located in Washington, DC. This emphasizes the fact that is an essential part of one of the three branches of government. Further, the fact that the Supreme Court is located in the District of Columbia means that if you are appealing a case to the Supreme Court, you must travel to the District of Columbia if the court agrees to hear the case.

Judicial Review

The biggest power of the United States Supreme Court is judicial review: the ability of the Court to review decisions made by lower courts at every level, as well as its ability to review both state and federal statutes. Because the Supreme Court can review any decision, it has the final say on how things are decided and on how laws should be interpreted. For example, if the Supreme Court rules that abortion must be legal based on its view of the Constitution, then no other state court can challenge that ruling of the Supreme Court and must abide by it unless or until the legislature changes the rules or another case gets to the Supreme Court and the Supreme Court changes its mind.

Court of Last Resort

In the United States criminal justice system, a court of last resort is the final court to which a matter can be appealed. Once a matter is appealed by the final appellate court, the decision made by the appellate court stands and cannot be altered, revised, or modified. For example, once a party has appealed to the US Supreme Court and the Supreme Court decides the case, then the party can no longer appeal the ruling. Since the Supreme Court takes only select cases (based on a writ of certiorari), the court of last resort is often the appellate court in either the state or federal system.

State Court Administrator

A state court administrator helps to manage case flow, administers court dockets, and assists in ensuring uninterrupted funding for a court. Because there is often a backlog of cases that judges and courts must deal with, it is important that someone has the job of keeping the docket organized and determining what cases will be heard, by whom, and when. It is imperative that these state court administrators be impartial, especially when assigning which case will be heard by which judge. Most states, but not all, use state court administrators to help make sure things run smoothly in the court system.

Minor Dispute Settlement

A dispute might be settled by an arbitrator at a dispute resolution center or a mediation center. These may often help to lessen the caseload of lower courts. Mediation is often a voluntary process, wherein the parties agree to try to work out their differences themselves. They have to pay a mediator to help them, and the mediator doesn't actually make any decisions—he just facilitates the parties making a decision. On the other hand, arbitration is required when the parties involved have signed an arbitration clause. A decision by an arbitrator is legally binding on the parties that submitted the issue to arbitration.

Trial Courts

The trial courts in the federal system are known as district courts. These are the lowest courts in the federal system, and they hear cases that arise out of federal law. These may be cases such as those based on federal legislation, such as Title VII, which is a federal law that prohibits discrimination against people based on race, gender, national origin, and religion. When a federal district court makes a decision, it can be appealed to only the federal appellate court in the relevant district—not to a state court.

Federal Courts

Federal courts have the initial jurisdiction over all cases that involve violation of federal statutes. This means that if a case arises out of federal law, it can be heard in federal court. Examples of federal law include the US bankruptcy code, the US tax code, and various pieces of environmental protection legislation and anti-discrimination legislation. When a federal court has jurisdiction, it may have exclusive or concurrent jurisdiction. Exclusive jurisdiction means that the federal court is the only court that can hear it, while concurrent jurisdiction means a state court could also decide that particular issue.

Regional Circuits

There are 12 regional circuits and 94 districts (or 89 districts counting the states only). Each of these districts governs a specific geographical area. If you live within a specific jurisdictional area and you wish to bring a case within the appropriate federal court, then you will need to make sure you bring the case within the appropriate district. This is important because of the concept of personal matter jurisdiction: If the federal court does not have jurisdiction based on where the person lives, then the court may not hear the case. There are fewer federal appellate courts, however, so if you need to appeal, you may need to travel a longer distance to have your case heard.

Appeals

The United States Constitution guarantees the right of an individual to appeal to a higher court. As such, federal circuit courts may experience an ever-increasing load of appeals to consider in keeping with the provision of the constitution. Either plaintiffs or defendants are able to appeal a decision that does not go in their favor. However, each party has the right to appeal to only one higher court. The US Supreme Court is not required to hear appeals, unless it chooses to do so. To file an appeal with the US Supreme Court, the individual would have to file a writ of certiorari and the Court would have to decide that the case was important enough to hear it.

Courtroom Work Group

A courtroom work group is the body consisting of all of the officials of a court, including the judge, prosecuting and defending attorneys (including public defenders), and anyone else whose occupation is serving the court. Each individual member of the courtroom work group serves an important role within the justice system. The prosecutor prosecutes criminals, while the defense attorneys work to ensure that those accused individuals receive a fair trial and are truly innocent until proven guilty. Without the entirety of the courtroom work group, the US justice system would be unable to function as intended by the Constitution, and rights would be in jeopardy.

Judges

Selection

In the United States, judges may be either elected or appointed. Most state court judges, especially at the lower level, are elected by the citizens. Judges who are elected serve for a set term of years (depending on the state) and then may run for reelection. US Supreme Court justices are all appointed by the President and they serve for a lifetime term. The purpose of this is to ensure that Supreme Court justices are impartial, while the purpose of electing state court judges is to ensure that they make and interpret laws based on the sentiments of the people within the state. While judges' first obligation is to uphold the law, no matter whether they are elected or appointed, judges who are elected also tend to cater as much as possible to the platform that got them elected.

Roles

Judges may have numerous roles. They preside over courts of law, hear and decide cases, and conduct trials. Some judges are responsible for hiring staff, scheduling court sessions, ensuring the training of lower judges, and coordinating activities with and for the other actors. The main role of the judge, however, is to ensure that the law is upheld or enforced. Judges do not get to interject their personal feelings of right or wrong in a case—they must do what the law says and uphold the law as written and interpreted by the courts above them.

Prosecutor

This is the prosecutor—also known as the district attorney, state attorney, county attorney, or solicitor. Prosecutors are responsible for conducting criminal proceedings. Only a prosecutor can bring criminal charges against an individual—private citizens are relegated to seeking justice through civil suits. Prosecutors have a sworn duty to the court to uphold the law and the principles of justice and can prosecute only those who they truly and honestly believe are guilty and deserving of facing criminal sanctions. There are usually several levels of prosecutors, such as the district attorney, assistant district attorney, and on down the line, all of whom work together to prosecute cases.

Prosecutorial Discretion

Prosecutorial discretion is the power of prosecutors to make decisions on the basis of the choices available to them. In other words, a prosecutor does not necessarily have to try every case that comes before him. He may decide which cases he has sufficient evidence for, whether he believes in the guilt of the accused, and whether it is in the interests of justice to prosecute the case. At times, the prosecutor also has discretion to prosecute even if the victim of the crime does not want him to. This is common in cases of domestic violence.

Defense Attorney

This is the defense attorney (or defense counsel), who is hired to defend those who are accused of crimes. The purpose of defense attorneys within the system is to ensure that all defendants have their constitutional right to a fair trial. Defense attorneys attempt to introduce reasonable doubt or raise affirmative defenses such as insanity to get a client off for crimes that were committed. Defense attorneys also ensure that law enforcement officials do not use illegal tactics, like illegal searches or coerced confessions, to put a person in prison. It is important to have defense attorneys to ensure that no innocent people are punished and that only the guilty have to face criminal sanctions.

Retained counsel, court-appointed counsel, and public defenders are the three categories of defense attorneys within the US system. Retained counsel are hired by those who pay privately. A person can choose any attorney he wants to defend him. Retained counsel often charge the most money and are typically higher-profile attorneys. For example, star defense lawyers such as those who defend famous celebrity criminals are often retained counsel. Public defenders are those who are appointed when people are unable to afford an attorney of their own.

Court-Appointed Attorneys and Public Defenders

Many decisions have reinforced the fact that the poor will be afforded defense attorneys even if they lack the ability to pay for them. Court-appointed attorneys and public defenders are two of the professionals employed to provide these individuals with legal defense. Anytime a person requests an attorney after being charged with a crime, the court must appoint a lawyer for him or her. This is done to ensure that all defendants get a fair trial and get their day in court, as guaranteed by the US Constitution.

Bailiff

A bailiff, the officer who keeps order in a courtroom, must also announce the judge's entry into the courtroom, call witnesses to testify, and ensure the safety of the accused, as well as ensure that the accused does not escape. Bailiffs may be armed and may be responsible for securing criminals or dealing with problems that may arise in a courtroom.

LAW

According to *Policing in America*, a law is a binding rule that regulates conduct and provides sanctions for violations of its provisions. There are several different types of laws: moral laws and ethical laws. Not all laws are enforced by the government. Only those that are made by the courts, the legislature, or the executive branch of the government are enforced by the courts. However, there is often much overlap between moral law and legal rules. For example, moral law would dictate that it is morally wrong to murder and thus that one should not kill. The legal system and the laws of the United States also prohibit murder, and it is penalized in the court system.

JURISDICTION

Jurisdiction is the territory over which an authority may exercise its power, as determined by laws or the constitution. For example, in order to make a law, the legislature must have jurisdiction over the issue or must have the power to make the law based on the Constitution. Courts too must have both subject-matter jurisdiction and personal jurisdiction to make a ruling in a case. For example, if a court is to hear a case, the defendant(s) must have sufficient ties with the court for it to be fair for the court to make a decision on what happens to the individual(s).

POLICE FORCE AND THE BRANCHES OF CONSTITUTIONAL GOVERNMENT

The US government has three branches: executive, legislative, and judicial. These branches of government ideally function independently of one another and keep one another in check, effecting the "separation of powers." The purpose of separation of powers is to make sure that no one branch of government abuses its power. As such, there are checks and balances built into the system. For example, a Supreme Court can overrule a law made by the legislature if the Supreme Court determines that the law is in violation of the US Constitution. A police force fulfills the will of all branches of government, although a police force comes under the power of the executive branch.

POLICE OFFICER

The primary function of a police officer is to protect and to serve the public. Police officers are required as well to act as officers and servants of the law. They may not abuse their position or make decisions that are in accordance with what they personally believe is right or wrong. They are bound to obey the Constitution as well as all the laws passed in their state and their locality. This means that police cannot subject citizens to unreasonable search and seizure, harass citizens, coerce confessions, or otherwise do anything in violation of their obligation to protect and to serve the public.

Law enforcement officers must often serve as animal control officials, water meter readers, home inspectors, and many other different functions throughout a regular day of work. The role of law enforcement officers depends on what their level is within the police force. Inspectors and detectives, for example, do very different work than those assigned to animal control or to patrol duty. While those who join the force do have some discretion regarding what job they do, ultimately it is up to their captain and superiors to decide how that particular officer can best serve the public.

FUNCTION AND ROLE

Police officers' functions are simply the tasks and activities associated with their roles. Roles are the basic positions held by police officers in society. Each role of a police officer carries with it a set of expectations that must be met for an officer to fill that role. Sometimes functions and roles overlap, but in every case, police officers must ensure that they fulfill both their roles in society and their functions within the police force and within the structure of the law enforcement and judicial system as a whole.

As social problems change, the roles of police adapt. Throughout history, they have variously functioned in crime fighting, public relations, and service roles. As technology evolves, police officers also begin to serve different functions. They may investigate different crimes that did not exist before, such as computer crimes and identity theft. They may also make use of new technologies like DNA forensics to investigate crimes. However, although the function of police officers may change and evolve, the emphasis on protecting life, liberty, and property will ensure that the police function remains intact no matter how the roles might change in the future.

The four main roles of a police officer are:

- To maintain order (this is done by patrolling, breaking up disorderly crowds or riots, and otherwise stopping behavior that disturbs the public)
- To enforce the law (this is done by investigating crimes and arresting the perpetrators)
- To provide services to the public (there are any number of services police can perform. One example of such services is attendance at safety events at schools to teach children how to protect themselves from crime)
- To enforce "convenience norms" (this too involves helping the public to ensure that there are no disturbances—for instance, issuing traffic citations)

Duties

When enforcing the law, a police officer may investigate a murder or other open case, serve a warrant, and question a suspect about a crime. Each police officer serves a different function within the system of the police force, depending on his rank and his particular assignment. For example, those who are assigned to patrol are typically out on the streets, looking for potential crimes or criminals and acting as a deterrent for those who are considering breaking the law. On the other hand, those who are detectives don't typically work the streets unless they are out investigating a specific case and interviewing witnesses.

Maintaining Order

Police officers maintain order in many ways. They may break up fights or riots in the street, step in when a party or concert gets out of hand, or investigate a domestic dispute. Police officers may arrest a person for disorderly conduct or for public intoxication. They may direct traffic in the event that a traffic light is out. Essentially, the function and role of a police officer is to make sure that life goes along smoothly for citizens and that their constitutional right to life, liberty, and the pursuit of happiness is protected.

Miscellaneous Services

Officers are often called on to look for missing persons, provide assistance in a medical emergency, and help people whose cars have broken down. Typically, police officers have some limitations on how some of these services may be provided. For example, in most cases, police will not investigate a missing persons report until the person in question has been missing for 24 hours. The purpose of these limitations is to ensure that police officers serve where they are most needed, since there tends to be more demand for police services than there is a supply of police officers to perform those services.

CONVENIENCE NORMS

The convenience-norms role of a police officer includes directing traffic, issuing traffic citations, and investigating and reporting on vehicular accidents. These tasks are an important role of police officers to help maintain public order and to make sure the streets and communities are safe. Imagine what would happen if a red light went out and there was no one there to direct traffic—police officers step up to the plate in such a situation to ensure that life can continue as normal for the people within the community.

STATE POLICE AGENCY AND HIGHWAY PATROL AGENCY

State police agencies have the powers of traffic regulation and criminal investigation, while highway patrol agencies have the authority to enforce traffic regulation and arrest nontraffic violators within their jurisdictions.

TRIBAL POLICE

Native American tribes often have criminal justice systems on their reservations, including tribal police forces that are separate from the US criminal justice system. Because Native American tribes are viewed as separate from the US and subject to separate laws, many standard state court systems do not have jurisdiction over tribal events and are not able to enforce tribal laws on the reservations. The function of tribal police, therefore, is to maintain law and order where US standard police forces and police officials do not have jurisdiction to go.

MUNICIPAL POLICE

Municipal police are the officers responsible for dealing with crime, order maintenance, and emergency services. They respond to 911 calls and requests for help within their local towns and communities, acting as the front line for service. They are arguably the most important component of law enforcement within the United States, since they can respond to people as needed to help protect against crime and ensure that law and order is enforced and upheld within cities and towns.

SHERIFFS AND CONSTABLES

Sheriffs must serve in law enforcement, courts, and corrections. In 37 states, it is a constitutional office. Constables typically work within county court systems, serving warrants, transporting prisoners, and working as security for judges. Some sheriffs and constables are considered to be law enforcement officials similar to police officers, while others have more limited power. The specific role of sheriffs and constables can vary depending on the state where the person in question is employed. In any situation, however, the primary function and underlying duty is to help uphold law and order and justice.

ROLES OF FEDERAL LAW ENFORCEMENT AGENCIES

The roles of federal law enforcement agencies are established by federal statute. This means that the roles are defined by the legislature that creates the particular federal law enforcement agency. Because the US Constitution vests all power in the states unless that power is expressly granted to the federal government, a federal law enforcement agency cannot exist without a derivative grant of power from the legislature that created it. In other words, the legislature must have the right to make and enforce the particular law or rule, and it passes that right and power on to the federal law enforcement agency it creates.

COMMUNITY CORRECTIONS

Community corrections is a style of sentencing criminals based on the correctional resources in a community. In other words, a community may have a limited number of jails or may have specific rehabilitation programs and criminal justice programs in place within the state. Common examples are states that use special programs for DUI and drug offenders to try to keep these offenders out of jail and explore alternative means of sentencing. Part of the aim of community corrections is to help establish a way to rehabilitate, whenever possible, those who live in a community so that career criminals do not become drains on that community's resources.

PROBATION

Probation is a sentence that is served by a criminal under supervision in a community. It uses community programs to attempt to rehabilitate these individuals. Probation is generally set for a term of years and can be used either as the sole sentence or can be used after a term in prison. Generally, probation violations result in re-incarceration, so it is imperative for those who are given a term of probation to avoid getting into any further trouble. The probation requirements will be set by the judge who sentences the individual. For example, probation for a DUI might include the requirement not to drink at all.

PAROLE

Parole is the supervised release of criminals after they have served a jail sentence. The concept of parole is important to help increase the chances that a criminal will not re-offend. There are many statistics that suggest that those who are in prison will wind up back in prison upon their release. By having to check in with a parole officer, the hope is that the person will be deterred from further criminal action. Parole officers may also check to make sure that paroled individuals are fulfilling the conditions of their release and may help to facilitate reentry into society by working with parolees to find jobs or develop skills for employment.

CORRECTIONS OFFICERS

Corrections officers, also known as prison wardens or detention officers, are responsible for caring for individuals who are incarcerated. The Eighth Amendment of the US Constitution prohibits cruel and unusual punishment of US citizens, and correctional officers are vested with the task of making sure that prisoners are safe and not subject to attacks or constitutional violations of their rights. They also maintain order in prisons to ensure that dangerous violent situations do not erupt and that dangerous criminals are not able to escape and get back on the streets.

RESPONSIBILITIES

Corrections officers must maintain peace and order in a correctional facility, search inmates for hidden drugs or weapons, respond to riots or other incidents of disorder, and transport inmates to and from the facility. The purpose is to ensure that no inmate's constitutional rights are violated, such as the prohibition against cruel and unusual punishment. The purpose is also to make sure that jails remain as safe as possible, given that there are a large number of criminals locked up in one place.

MODERN JUSTICE PROCESS

The modern criminal justice process begins with the investigation of an alleged crime. Typically, this occurs when a victim comes forward and reports a crime or when a victim is found, such as a dead body. An investigator or detective will be assigned to the case and he may work with a forensics team and a medical examiner to gather evidence. He may also interview witnesses, check financial records, and otherwise take any and all steps to determine what occurred and who perpetrated the crime. However, during the investigation process, it is imperative that all constitutional rights, including the right to privacy, are respected.

After a thorough investigation to determine who is responsible for committing the crime in question, the police department must obtain a warrant—a judicial directive for an officer to perform a specified action and protection from damages that may occur—to arrest the individual. Warrants can be obtained only with sufficient evidence to arrest the individual for the crime and are usually obtained by a prosecutor who uses the information from the police to convince a judge or a grand jury that a warrant for arrest should be issued.

MIRANDA RIGHTS

People are initially told their rights when they are questioned as suspects by the police. These rights are widely called the Miranda rights, based on a Supreme Court case wherein it was mandated that all suspects be read their rights before questioning. The police must respect these rights, so once suspects in custody ask for a lawyer, the police may no longer question them until the lawyer is present. Suspects are then once again read their rights during booking, when their detention and arrest are recorded.

BAIL

Money pledged or paid to a court for a person's release from legal custody is referred to as *bail*. The purpose is to make sure the person returns to court for actual trial. Bail may be posted using collateral, such as a home, or using cash. There are also individuals called bail bondsmen who will post bail for an accused after obtaining sufficient collateral from that individual and his or her family members. Bail is offered in certain cases to ensure that a people do not remain in prison pending trial but to still guarantee their return.

PRELIMINARY HEARING

A preliminary must determine

- Whether a crime was committed (i.e., whether a specific law has been broken)
- Whether the crime occurred within the court's jurisdiction (does the court have the right to enforce the law that was broken? State courts, for example, can enforce state laws, while federal courts can enforce federal laws)
- Whether reason exists (probable cause) to believe the defendant was the individual who committed the crime. This can be determined by DNA evidence, witness statements, a confession, or anything else that provides sufficient information to suggest that there is a reasonable possibility that the defendant was guilty of the crime. This is not a full trial, it just needs to be proven that there is a reason to believe that the person did something wrong and will be found guilty during the process of a full trial.

INDICTMENT

An indictment is a written accusation submitted to a court by the grand jury, a group of individuals who have sworn to hear the evidence and determine whether a person may be brought to trial. The purpose of an indictment is to determine whether there is sufficient evidence to bring a person to trial for a crime he has allegedly committed. This is not the same as needing to convince the grand jury that the defendant is guilty—that will be done at trial. This is just to convince the grand jury that there is enough reason to believe the person is guilty that he should be subject to a full trial to determine guilt or innocence.

ARRAIGNMENT

The first appearance of defendants before the court where they will be tried is called the arraignment. At the arraignment, the charges against defendants are read to them. Defendants are able to plead either guilty or not guilty. If they are pleading not guilty, they can assert an affirmative defense at this time. Examples of an affirmative defense include self-defense or insanity. Bail is generally decided at arraignment as well. Guilt or innocence is not determined—the arraignment simply sets the stage for the trial that will come later, where guilt or innocence will be determined.

SENTENCES

Those convicted of crimes may receive a *consecutive* sentence, where multiple sentences are served separately in sequence; or a *concurrent* sentence, where multiple sentences are served all at the same time. Typically, a consecutive sentence is given when there are circumstances that lead the sentencing judge to believe that the individual requires a longer term of imprisonment in order to be rehabilitated or in order to ensure public safety.

DUE PROCESS

Due process is, very simply defined, a right of procedural fairness in a court of law. Due process ensures that no rights of defendants are violated. These rights include the right to have the Miranda warnings read to them, the right against unreasonable search and seizure, and the right to a speedy trial. Due process, therefore, ensures that the process by which a person is investigated, tried, and convicted is fair and that no person is deprived of life, liberty, or the pursuit of happiness without a trial in an unbiased court.

UCR

The UCR, Uniform Crime Report, is a compilation, proposed by Vollmer, of crime statistics as tracked throughout the United States. It focuses on "index" crimes, and is a popular method for classifying, measuring, and assessing crime to determine whether police action is required in a certain area.

The Green Book, or UCR Handbook, is published by the FBI as an aid to officers in filling out UCR reports correctly. Filling out the reports properly is a key function of a police officer's job, as the reports allow for the creation of important statistics that are used to determine where a greater police presence may be necessary, as well as where police techniques for deterring crime have been most effective. Since the UCR reports are key to public policy decisions, they must be filled out correctly and in a uniform manner from police officer to police officer. The handbook helps to ensure this.

NCVS

The National Crime Victimization Survey comprises data from households throughout the United States to determine the frequency of crime victimization, police response, and other factors to help measure and understand crime across the country.

NIBRS

The National Incident Based Reporting System is a method employed by law enforcement agencies in the United States to collect and report crime data year after year. The purpose is to determine what crime fighting tactics and police strategies are effective. The statistics are also used to determine where a larger police presence may be necessary. Many private individuals use the statistics to determine where to live and whether a neighborhood is safe. Thus, the NIBRS has an unintended effect on property values as well as serving an important law enforcement role.

REASONABLE DOUBT

In a criminal proceeding, reasonable doubt is a substantial doubt arising from the facts demonstrated by the evidence. It is a standard of proof necessary for the conviction of a criminal in the justice system. A prosecutor must prove guilt beyond a reasonable doubt, i.e., he must prove conclusively that the defendant committed the crime. He does not have to prove that there is 100 percent certainty that the defendant is guilty, since that would be an impossible standard. He does, however, have to prove that there is no doubt that the defendant did it. The reason the standard is set so high is to ensure that no innocent people end up having to serve a term in prison.

Interpretation of Rights

While the Constitution does determine basic human rights, rights are also based on interpretation and owe much to the Supreme Court's determination of what rights are and how they are to function in American society. In other words, because the Constitution cannot cover every eventuality, it must be interpreted. Other laws are also imperfect or incomplete and must be interpreted or defined by the courts that are in place to enforce those laws. Ultimately, this means that rights are a conglomeration of constitutional law, legislation, and common law made by the courts and judges.

Crime Control Model of Justice

The crime control model focuses specifically on the arrest and conviction of criminals. In other words, the focus is simply on finding a person who is responsible for committing a crime and on prosecuting that person for the crime so that the person may be incarcerated. This is often viewed as taking a hard stance on crime and criminals and can act as a strong deterrent to individuals who are involved with police forces using the crime control model of justice.

Due Process Model of Justice

Unlike the crime-control model of justice, which is concerned primarily with arrest and conviction, the due process model of justice emphasizes the importance of the rights of an individual throughout the justice process. The main aim here is not just to find, arrest, and convict criminals, but to make sure that every person's full and complete constitutional rights are protected to the fullest extent possible. This model of justice is willing to sacrifice convictions and allow some guilty people to walk free in order to make sure that the innocent are fully protected.

Criminology

The scientific study of the causes and prevention of criminal acts and the punishment and rehabilitation of those convicted is called criminology. Criminology involves looking at how and why people commit crimes. Criminology also looks at which methods are most and least effective at deterring crimes and rehabilitating criminals. The purpose of criminologists is to reduce the crime rate by gathering data for a better understanding of the means to reduce crime and of why crime is committed in the first place.

Victimology

Victimology is the study of the process of victimization, a subfield of criminology. It, too, aims to understand the role of criminals and victims within the context of a crime. The main focus of this is to understand how and why people become victims and to stop that from occurring by better understanding the criminal process.

Police Systems in the United States

Federal Law Enforcement Agencies

Federal law enforcement agencies are charged by the United States government with enforcing federal laws. Federal laws apply to interstate crime and organized crime through such legislation as the Racketeer-Influenced and Corrupt Organizations (RICO) Act. Mail fraud is another example of a federal crime. These are distinct from crimes that are controlled on a state level, such as murder and theft. When a crime is at federal level, only the federal courts can prosecute those indicted for it. Another classic example is tax fraud—a state court cannot prosecute offenders who violate the US tax code, since that is left exclusively to the province of the federal tax courts and federal law enforcement agencies.

Employment of Law Enforcement Officers

Thirteen government agencies employ law enforcement officers—the Department of Agriculture, the Department of Commerce, the Department of Defense, the Department of Homeland Security, the Department of the Interior, the Department of Justice, the Department of Labor, the Department of State, the Department of Transportation, the Department of the Treasury, and the Postal Service, the Food and Drug Administration, and the US Mint. The Capitol Police, the Forest Service, the National Park Service, and the Fish and Wildlife Service are among the organizations that employ hundreds (if not thousands) of full-time law enforcement officers. These agencies are responsible for serving a number of important roles. For example, those who are employed in the national parks help to make sure that the rules of the park are enforced. They assist in making sure people do not litter, take things from the parks, or otherwise do actions that would destroy the beauty and integrity of the parks that are there for everyone's enjoyment. The Fish and Wildlife Service, on the other hand, issues hunting licenses. Its role is to keep the population of hunted game at appropriate levels.

FBI

The Federal Bureau of Investigation, the FBI, is perhaps the most well known law enforcement agency in the world. The FBI provides a centralized bank of intelligence that is designed to collect information on criminals throughout all 50 US states. This information is used to investigate crimes at both federal and state levels, and the FBI often works in cooperation or conjunction with state law enforcement agencies to investigate federal crimes that occur within a given state. The FBI also publishes a 10 Most Wanted list of criminals that it most needs to apprehend. There is generally a reward for those who turn in information that leads to the capture and arrest of a person who is on the FBI's 10 Most Wanted list.

In 1908, the Bureau of Investigation was created as the investigative arm of the Department of Justice to help curb business corruption. Its name was changed to the Federal Bureau of Investigation. Because the FBI operates at the federal, as opposed to the state, level, the bureau was tasked with regulating interstate corruption and criminal activity that occurred across state lines. In fact, because the power was granted to the federal government in the Constitution to manage and govern interstate commerce, the states do not have authority to make rules or enforce laws on commercial transactions that occur across state lines. The FBI was created to fill that void and provide the necessary enforcement.

J. Edgar Hoover

John Edgar Hoover, a powerful and controversial figure served with the Bureau of Investigation and then the FBI from 1924 until his death in 1972. J. Edgar Hoover is responsible for expanding the role of the FBI and for making it the dominant force in federal law enforcement.

CIA

The Central Intelligence Agency (CIA) was established to gather information about the actions of foreign countries and to provide intelligence to the US government about foreign affairs. It is a federal agency, created under the authority of the federal government. Unlike the FBI, the CIA has limited authority to investigate matters taking place within the United States, but instead helps to manage the information necessary to secure the US from foreign powers that might want to do it harm.

The CIA was established in 1947, following the Second World War. Because of alliances formed in the Second World War and because of the realization that foreign nations and their adverse actions could have a strong impact on life in America, it became clear that the world was becoming a smaller place and that it was imperative for the US to have information on the actions of those in foreign countries, especially those who could be viewed as hostile to the United States. The CIA was created to collect this intelligence, monitor it, and be aware of any situations that might be developing that could pose a threat to the security of the United States.

September 11, 2001

After terrorists struck New York City and the Pentagon on September 11, 2001, the CIA was dramatically restructured, creating separate positions for the Director of National Intelligence and the Director of the CIA. The purpose was to provide a stronger law enforcement body to monitor new forms of intelligence. As terrorism evolves with new technologies, such as biological weapons and warfare, it has become essential that there be sufficient law enforcement personnel organized to monitor all information and be aware of any and all potential threats to national security that exist.

Treasury Department

The Treasury Department has several law enforcement agencies: The Bureau of Alcohol, Tobacco, and Firearms; the Internal Revenue Service; the US Secret Service; and formerly the US Customs Service. Each of these departments has a different set of duties. For example, the Secret Service is best known for its role in protecting the President. The Internal Revenue service collects income tax and monitors citizens for tax evasion. The income taxes collected by the IRS are essential to the function of the country, as they are used for important government programs and to pay down the ever-growing national debt.

BATF

As its name indicates, some of the responsibilities of the BATF include curbing the traffic and use of illegal firearms, regulating alcohol, tobacco, and explosives industries, ensuring collection of revenue from the sale of tobacco and firearms, and investigating any violations of federal explosives laws.

IRS

By far, the Internal Revenue Service (IRS) is the largest bureau of the Treasury Department. Because every American citizen is required to file income tax, a very large governing body is necessary to enforce the laws relating to it. The US tax code is also a very large and complex document and many IRS officials are required to enforce the rules set within the document and to help with interpreting the code. Those who work for the IRS perform a number of functions, including monitoring tax returns, identifying potential tax evasion, and auditing those who may not be paying the full amount of income taxes owed to the government. Catching those who evade their tax obligation is essential to collect lost revenue and to deter others who might be tempted to cheat on their taxes.

US Customs Service and the Department of Homeland Security

The former bureau that was responsible for collecting tariffs and securing the borders of the US was the US Customs Service, which was dissolved and combined with the Department of Homeland Security. The function of this bureau is to ensure that no one enters the United States without proper authority and permission. Not only does this involve taking action to deter illegal immigration and "border jumpers" (as those who try to cross the border illegally are often called), but it also involves taking the proper steps to make sure that goods and items entering the United States are taxed appropriately. Since tariffs are used to regulate trade as well, this department serves an important role within the US economy in addition to serving an important national security role.

Secret Service

Originally, the intent of the Secret Service was to capture counterfeiters. In 1901, the Secret Service began providing protection for the President following the assassination of President McKinley. Today, this is the job that the Secret Service is best known for. As soon as individuals begin to run for the presidential office, they are typically afforded Secret Service protection. This protection occurs during the duration of the time the President is in office and may continue following his term of service as well. Those who are in the Secret Service are sworn to protect the President, even by giving their own lives if necessary.

State Police Agencies

Initially, state police organizations were formed to help aid local police forces, to enforce the law in rural areas, and to deal with interboundary criminal activities. They served as helpful assistance and enforcers of the law in areas where there was not a significant enough police presence. As such, they acted as important deterrents against those who were committing crimes that the police could not necessarily respond to. In rural areas especially, it could become difficult for police who might have a wide jurisdiction to enforce all laws at disparate homes and communities spread wide apart.

First All-Purpose State Police Organization

The Pennsylvania State Police (PSP), created in response to the Anthracite Coal Strike of 1902, was the first all-purpose state police organization. Pennsylvania at this time was facing a great deal of political turmoil and strife, in large part because of poor working conditions and problems between the miners in the coal mines and those working in factories. Because there was no organized state police organization at the time of the strike, there was no way to respond to the violence that ensued or to quash the violent actions that were occurring. The PSP was created to help to resolve the problems between the factory workers and the miners as well as the problems that occurred as a result of the strike.

Investigative Agencies

Many states with highway patrols also employ investigative agencies. These investigative agencies help to identify offenses that were committed and to find those who were guilty of law violations. They serve an important role both in identifying those who commit crimes so that they may be brought to justice and in acting as a deterrent. In states where investigative agencies exist, the people are aware that there is this additional body of law enforcement officials, and this can help to deter potential wrongdoers from breaking the law.

Limited-Purpose State Law Enforcement Agencies

Some states created specialized police forces to meet special law enforcement needs. Peace officers, fish and game warden organizations, and Alcoholic Beverage Control Commissions are among the most common. Fish and game warden organizations, for example, set the dates when hunting season is open on various types of game. They also issue hunting and fishing licenses and taxes that allow individuals to catch and capture only a certain amount of wildlife. Their purpose is to make sure that populations such as that of deer neither get out of control and become destructive nor become overhunted in a given area.

Local Law Enforcement Agencies

Local law enforcement agencies employ the most individuals. This is true because the vast majority of crimes are governed at the state level. For example, murder, theft, robbery, assault, domestic violence, drug convictions, alcohol convictions, and numerous other felonies and misdemeanors are all governed under state law and the statutes and rules are enforced by local law enforcement agencies. With so many more rules to enforce than the federal government has, it is no wonder that there are many more state and local police required compared with other law enforcement agencies.

Sheriff's Departments and County Police Organizations

Both of these are employed at the county level. This means that they report to local police forces and answer to the local officials, such as the chief of police. They are, of course, ultimately obligated to obey all federal laws and to enforce the rules set forth in the Constitution. Still, while their ultimate duty is to the United States as a whole, their daily duties are governed by responding to the needs and directives of the local elected law enforcement officials in the areas where they are employed.

NYPD

The New York City Police Department (NYPD) is the largest municipal police department in the United States. The city of New York is densely populated and used to have a reputation for having a very high crime rate. Reform efforts resulted in more police being brought to New York City in an effort to deal with the crime problems running rampant in the city. Today, crime in New York is more under control than it was in the past and the city has become safer. Still, the concentrated area of people, and the wide discrepancies between the very wealthy and the poor in New York City necessitate a large police force to keep order.

Special District Police Agencies

Special district police agencies have authority only in certain areas. For instance, colleges, airports, public schools, transportation systems, public housing, and government buildings might all employ law enforcement agents. These law enforcement agencies may have only a limited set of rights and duties. For example, college police officials may have the authority to enforce college rules, but typically will not be enforcing the major rules of the state or of the United States itself. This means a college police official may deal with a parking violation on campus, but if he suspects that one of the students he is responsible for monitoring has committed a serious crime such as a rape or murder, he will generally call in official law enforcement personnel rather than handle it himself, since it is not within his jurisdiction or grant of power.

Small Town Law Enforcement Services

In general, police officers often have to perform more public service than law enforcement in smaller towns—jobs considered outside of police responsibility may need to be performed in smaller or rural jurisdictions. For example, police may provide private security at large public events. They may rescue a cat out of a tree. These are not essential to fighting crime, of course, but these extra services can help to ensure that a community runs smoothly and that there is a good relationship maintained between the police and the people living in a given city or area.

Roles of Police Officers

Police officers may have many different roles during the course of their job. Maintaining order and control, enforcing the law, serving citizens, and enforcing norms are all among the roles of police officers. Depending on location, situation, and culture, the roles may vary. The roles of police officers may also vary depending on their position within the police force and the police organization. Ultimately, however, no matter what role officers are serving, their underlying duty and most important role is to protect the rights of all citizens and to uphold the law in everything they do.

Ultimately, everything that the police officer does is done toward this aim. Police can enforce the law by making their presence known so that they may act as a deterrent for those who are considering breaking the law. They may enforce the law by investigating to determine who committed a crime so that the person can be brought to justice. In every step of enforcing the law, the police officer must also obey the law. This means respecting the constitutional rights of every person under investigation and making sure that investigation methods or other tasks are performed within the bounds of their duties and within the constraints of all laws.

Day to Day Roles and Assignments

Many people may be responsible for determining the role of a police officer. City councils, mayors, and local governments will often determine the role of a police officer within a particular jurisdiction. Usually, each police officer is given orders and commanded to do certain activities by his superior or commanding officer, the person who is directly above him. The chief of police, for example, will dictate to captains of police precincts what those captains are supposed to do. The captains will then give assignments to their subordinates, including the investigators and detectives working under him.

Prescribed Roles

Prescribed roles are the tasks required by law for police officers to perform. These are the basic tasks that are the essential functions of a police officer's job description. They can vary depending on what a particular police officer's role is. For example, detectives have prescribed roles to solve the particular crimes that they are assigned to and will do everything within their legal authority to solve those crimes. Police may sometimes have to do tasks outside of their prescribed roles, such as helping victims to get the strength to testify about what happened to them. This is not technically the job of police officers, but it is sometimes done by them anyway.

Ethics

It is not advisable for a law enforcement officer to use "dirty" means to accomplish an ultimately worthwhile goal. The ethical lines of a police officer should not be blurred—in other words, the ends generally do not justify the means. If a police officer does something improper or incorrect in order to accomplish his goal, this creates a number of problems. It undermines community trust in the police force. It can also result in the case not being brought to trial and the criminal not being brought to justice, since a court will not hear evidence that has been illegally or improperly obtained. Finally, it is in direct contrast to the ultimate duty of a police officer, which is to uphold and to enforce the law.

Organization, Management, and Issues

Basic Organizational Types in Police Forces

Line operations and staff operations are the two main organizational types. Each of these organizational types is essential to keep a police force running smoothly. *Line operations* involve the basic, required, everyday tasks of police officers. This is the police work that the public sees. Line operations are transmitted through the lines of command—a police captain giving orders to his lieutenants and detectives, a watch commander sending officers out on patrol. *Staff operations,* on the other hand, do not come from the chain of command and do not involve doing the required tasks of officers on the street. Staff operations comprise the support staff of a police force—the administrators and others who are employed by a police force but are not "on the line" (i.e., doing line operations).

Staff structure allows individuals other than line managers to deal with budgeting, training, scientific analysis, and personnel management. This is essential because the managers or those on top of the line and in charge of issuing assignments and orders do not have time to deal with the practical details of running a police organization. Issues such as budgeting and paychecks are essential to keep the police organization running smoothly, but they must be done by the staff so that the police can concentrate on doing police work. In a line organization, however, only the line managers would be able to deal with decision making—even if that decision making was on things such as budgeting and training. This would detract from the job the line manager really should be doing.

Line Operations

Line operations are supervisory roles or field activities related to the day-to-day work of law enforcement personnel. It is imperative that the chain of command be followed appropriately and that the line operations be set forth in an organized manner. Without a proper chain of authority and a proper listing and description of operations and how the chain of authority and assignments will work, police officers would be unable to function and do their jobs. There would be chaos, crimes could be left unsolved, or dangerous emergencies unresponded to because there would be no clear chain of command or appropriate methods to resolve these issues. Line operations usually have a top-to-bottom flow of authority without supporting elements such as training and media relations—they exist to provide field services. In other words, the person who is at the top of the line structured organization is the person who is in charge. He hands out assignments, decides who does what and must be obeyed. There is little to no room on a police force for questioning orders or for not obeying a commanding officer. Since lives are at stake, it is very important that everyone is on the same page, knows what he or she is doing, and complies with the orders that are issued.

Staff Operations

Staff operations are support roles in law enforcement, such as administration and the like. Those who are not actually on the police force and who are not part of the major chain of command (such as captain and subordinates) are also an essential part of keeping the police force running smoothly. Because these individuals are not on the line doing police work every day, it is not as essential that they obey orders and maintain their job duties based on the line of command and their expected obligations. Yet, they still must be part of the team of those individuals providing police work, and they must provide appropriate support to those on the front lines.

Line-Only Organizations

Only the smallest police organizations are structured purely as "line" organizations. Typically a staff or support organization or structure must be part of the police force. Because the police must concentrate on doing police work, they do not have time to do the support work that a staff does. The staff can handle things such as budgeting for the police force, paying out salaries and otherwise taking care of the details not essential or necessary for solving crimes. This frees up the police officers to do the work they need to do to keep the streets safe. In a line-only organization, this staff does not exist and the police have to take time away from their main duties to keep a police force running structurally so it does not fall apart.

Staffing

Staffing refers to the responsibility of determining the recruitment, selection, and training of individuals for placement in a police organization or service. When police forces are staffed, it is essential to hire individuals who are qualified to do the dangerous and sometimes difficult work that must be done. This involves doing many things, including ensuring that the prospective police who are being hired are both physically and mentally fit. Typically, staff at a police force involves hiring recruits who must pass a background check, a series of psychological tests, and a program at the police academy before they can officially become police officers.

Span of Control

"Span of control" refers to the number of individuals at a supervisor's disposal or the number of units supervised by a commander. In other words, if a captain is in charge of the 12 people below him, then his span of control is 12 people. The larger the span of control a person has, the more responsibility he must take on for managing those who are below him.

Chain of Command

The hierarchy of any police organization is known as the "chain of command." Like in the military, there is a clear distinction for who reports to whom and who is in charge of whom. Also, like in the military, those who are lower down on the chain of command are expected to respect and follow the orders of those above them on the chain of command. Failure to do so could result in a disorganized police force that is unable to function. This could put lives in danger and create jeopardy for the public. It could also result in crimes not being solved.

Detectives

Police investigators were first called *detectives* in the 1840s, when the London Police created the world's first detective unit. The aim of this unit was the same as that of detective units today: to investigate crimes where the identity of the perpetrator or other information was unclear. These early efforts to solve crimes did not have many of the investigative techniques that are used today to collect evidence or to identify the guilty party, but the purpose was still the same and the early detectives of the London Police had some success in identifying and apprehending criminals.

While not universal, of course, police detectives were often unsavory individuals who themselves engaged in illicit activities. When they caught criminals, they were generally rewarded with accolades, recognition, and money. Many police selectively enforced the law or accepted bribes to look the other way when a crime was committed. There was a great deal of police corruption, some of which was known of by the general public and which contributed to creating a bad reputation. By the 1920s, however, this role began to change into today's investigative role.

Undercover

Detectives must often work clandestinely in order to infiltrate a criminal organization. Often, it is not easy to gather the required evidence against criminals to put them in prison. This is especially true for any type of organized crime ring, where the individuals involved are career criminals capable of sophisticated methods of eluding the police. As such, often detectives must operate in secret to infiltrate the ring from the outside in. This is called going undercover, in which a police officer will pose, for instance, as a drug runner or other criminal in order to become a part of the organization under investigation.

Change in Interrogation for the Better

Early interrogations were often brutal, and information and confessions were extracted from criminals by some violent means. There were limited or no protections in place to make sure that confessions were not coerced or forced out of individuals, even when those individuals were innocent. Detectives focused on inquisition and investigation to extract information in a much more humane way. Methods of torture and police coercion of confessions were eliminated in favor of creative methods of interrogation designed to do what was necessary to get the criminal talking. This might involve gaining a person's trust or baiting a person into confessing—but does not involve torture or coercion.

Investigations changed as a result of governments working to professionalize the police and because of the restraints placed on police investigations during the Civil Rights era of the 1960s. Police became more accountable to standards, in part to improve police/community relations. It became unacceptable to torture or coerce confessions or to look the other way when a crime was committed in order to receive a bribe. Those who were involved in fighting for civil rights also took steps to make sure that people under police custody were treated fairly so that there were no forced confessions, especially among the innocent.

Preliminary Investigation

A preliminary investigation is the initial inquiry into a crime that was allegedly committed and reported. A preliminary investigation may involve interviewing a complaining witness, reviewing the basic information about the crime, and ascertaining what law or laws were broken. A preliminary investigation generally does not involve searching for or interviewing witnesses (other than the person making the complaint and/or other witnesses actually at the scene and available to speak to immediately). Any other evidence gathering comes after a preliminary investigation has already been completed. Preliminary investigations usually last under an hour.

Walkthrough, Where-Are-They, and Whodunit

Walkthroughs are preliminary investigations done when a suspect is apprehended. In other words, if the police see someone committing a crime and they apprehend that person, they may do a walkthrough of what they saw and of what particular crime was committed. A where-are-they investigation means that officers are unable to make an arrest of an identified suspect. In other words, if the police are called to the scene of a crime and told who committed it but that person is not physically there to be arrested, it is considered a where-are-they investigation, and the aim is to find the person who has been identified as the perpetrator of the crime. Whodunits are cases where investigations did not turn up a perpetrator's identity. When the police are called to a scene of a crime and do not know who committed it, this is a whodunit.

Traffic Citations

The traffic function of police affects the greatest number of people yearly. More people become involved with the police through a traffic citation than through an arrest for any other crime. Traffic citations can include parking tickets, speeding tickets, reckless driving, or other charges that are solely traffic based. Driving Under the Influence (DUI), while a traffic offense, is also a separate criminal offense as well. Basic traffic cases (such as parking tickets and speeding tickets) are handled through the traffic courts, but many of these cases are pleaded out when the person pays the ticket and never actually involve the intervention of the courts at all.

Traffic Control Functions

Traffic control functions are carried out through regulation of traffic flow, enforcement of laws, and investigation of accidents. This means many things: If there is construction going on, the police may park their vehicles in the area both to flash their lights to warn people of the construction and to ticket those who do not obey speed laws. It can also mean directing traffic if a light is out. Laws are enforced through ticketing, such as issuing a speeding ticket when a person is found to exceed the legal posted speed limit; various methods, such as radar and laser detectors, are used to make such a determination. Finally, police go to the scene of the accident when they are called and make a report that is later used for insurance determinations.

Internal Affairs Division

Internal Affairs is usually responsible for proving any wrongdoing on the part of those within a specific department. The purpose is to help stop and prevent police corruption and to help ensure that the police are subject to laws and bound by the rules of the force. If there is a police officer suspected of misconduct, the Internal Affairs division will generally become involved in investigating that misconduct before any other official investigation is conducted as to whether a crime was committed or not. If the Internal Affairs division finds misconduct, it will deal with the police officer as it sees fit, by suspension, termination, or pursuing criminal sanctions if appropriate.

Anticorruption Efforts

Anticorruption efforts require help from a chief executive, a reasonable number of qualified personnel, and effective (centralized or decentralized) management). Corruption of the police force must be tackled from the inside out and must deal with the problems that occur because of abuses of police power. Often, it is hard to get police officers to turn in other police officers who have done something wrong. Thus, there must be widespread support for any anticorruption effort and it must be backed by those in charge if it is to be successful.

Influence of Research on Police Activity

Research helps officials understand and respond to trends in a changing policing climate. For example, if research indicates that crime rates are on the rise, it can be important to employ more police officials for a given location or area. Research can also give insight into criminal behavior and into new ways that laws can be enforced and crime can be deterred. In fact, research is such an important influence on police activity that the future will likely hold greater funding, although reduced support for research may prove to harm police research in perpetuity.

Crime Lab and the Lie Detector

August Vollmer is responsible for the introduction of both the crime lab and the lie detector. These two innovations have had a major impact on the way police work is conducted. The crime lab allows the prosecutor to identify DNA evidence and other information and to help police find out who committed a crime. Evidence acquired in a crime lab is also useful for making sure that the criminals are convicted. Lie detectors are not admissible in court but are still an important investigative tool that police sometimes use to eliminate suspects.

Foot Patrol and the Community

The police and citizenry are brought together in instances of foot patrol, which, according to studies, increases the feeling of safety among citizens. Foot patrol involves police officers going out and walking the streets of their "beat" or the neighborhood where they are assigned. This allows people to see a police presence in a community, which can deter crime. Since police are out and interacting with the public, it also helps to destroy myths and stereotypes about police and it helps to foster a relationship between the police and the people who live within the community they are patrolling.

Neighborhood Watch

While Neighborhoods Watches increase community participation, they have little effect on crime rates. Neighborhood Watch involves a group of citizens or neighbors coming together to patrol the streets to help deter crime and to help catch criminals. The Neighborhood Watch generally works closely with the police, setting up schedules with police approval and keeping the police on call in case a crime is found to be occurring during the Neighborhood Watch process. However, while Neighborhood Watch is effective at improving community relations, most criminal are not frightened by the authority of their neighborhood watch and thus are not deterred from their criminal actions.

Halfway Houses and Work-Release Programs

Halfway houses are places where a person or persons can live upon release from incarceration or upon release from a mental health facility. They provide a way for a person to become re-acclimated to life without the supervision and guidance of correction officers. Because a person has a place to live and rules to follow and is held accountable in the halfway house, it helps make it easier for her to establish a new role in society and to get back on track by getting a job and becoming a productive citizen. Work release programs also rely on the community to help with rehabilitation by allowing those who are in jail to be let out to go to work.

Community Interests and Innovative Police Programs

Unfortunately, sometimes community issues work against policing programs, if, for example, there is not widespread support for the particular community program and/or if the police are not able to work together with the community to achieve the desired aim. The community may also not be on board with the initiative—such as not being in support of a halfway house being found in their neighborhood. However, the COPS committee determined a decade ago that community policing strategies were often extremely effective.

African American Community and the Police in the 1960s

Unfortunately, the relationship between the police and minority groups during the Civil Rights movement was abrasive and contributed to the disorder. Police engaged in outright stereotyping and racial profiling, often harassing minorities simply because of their minority status. Police also perpetrated other abuses against African Americans, such as police brutality. The police in many locations were clearly anti-African American and this showed in their actions and in their treatment of many of the efforts of the early Civil Rights movement.

Initial Success of Police/Community Programs

No, they were not; rather, they were looked at as an attempt to whitewash policing institutions. The community did not respect the efforts of the police, nor did they believe the police were legitimately trying to improve relations between the community and the force. There was widespread distrust of the police and of the community efforts that were in place. However, through various partnerships over time, and through programs such as Neighborhood Watch efforts and initiatives, eventually police community programs became a generally successful endeavor that helped to foster a more positive relationship between the police and the communities the police were protecting.

COMMUNITY RELATIONS

Community relations reinforce service, citizens' rights, and order maintenance. Community relations help to improve the relationship between the police and the surrounding community so that there is greater cooperation from members of the community. This can help act as a further deterrent to criminal behavior and can facilitate citizen cooperation during investigations of various lawbreaking activities. Community relations also help allow the police to maintain an ordered environment within the given community so that people can enjoy their rights to life, liberty, and the pursuit of happiness without disorderly conduct interfering.

POLICE/COMMUNITY MODEL IN THE 1980S

While crime rates were falling, the media publicized crime throughout the period. Individuals became concerned about the rising tide of crimes, especially in major cities like New York. It began to be feared that a crime epidemic was occurring, resulting in a greater police presence in many areas. When the police presence grew, the police/community model also began to develop both as a way to increase positive interaction with police and community and to allow police greater opportunity to take action to quash the rising crime rates.

WAR ON DRUGS

The Reagan and first Bush administrations were largely responsible for creating the war on drugs. The war on drugs did several things. It criminalized certain drugs that had not previously been illegal and it encouraged enforcement of anti-drug laws by mandating state cooperation and by ensuring harsher penalties for those who were found guilty of drug offenses. There was also an education component where individuals were shown the danger that drugs could do. The combined efforts of all programs, including an increased law enforcement focus on apprehending drug offenders, was to eliminate drug abuse in the US. This effort has yet to be successful.

POLICE PATROL

A patrol is intended to enforce the law, deter crime, investigate unlawful activities, apprehend criminals, write reports, resolve conflicts, keep the peace, and maintain order. When police patrol an area, they usually go with a partner. The patrol can be either a foot patrol or can be done in a car, and the area the police are patrolling is sometimes referred to as their "beat." The patrol not only allows police to be made aware of anything out of the ordinary, but it also allows the community members to be aware that the patrol is going on. This deters crime and makes the police more of a positive public presence within the community.

Patrols may be carried out on horseback, from aircraft, by bike, or by watercraft. Police departments are often looking for creative ways to patrol that have advantages over more conventional methods of patrol. Helicopter patrol, for example, allows for the largest coverage, as police can scan a massive amount of area in a very brief period of time. However, helicopter patrol is less visible and is less of a crime deterrent, and it does not allow police to get to know a community or neighborhood. Each different method of patrol has advantages and disadvantages that must be weighed carefully when determining which method to use to patrol a given area.

Patrols were once done either on horseback or on foot. Those police officers on horses were able to cover more ground than police officers who were working on foot. Still, the police on both horseback and foot were able to get to know the people within the areas they were patrolling, and became familiar with the areas so that the officers would immediately be able to spot any signs that something was amiss. The fact that the beat was done on horseback or on foot allowed for an even greater connection with those on the beat than patrols done in cars, which is the way patrols are done today. Patrols done by car, however, allow police to cover much ground quickly and tend to be safer for the officer(s).

Foot patrol addresses the problem of decreased interaction between police and the public. When police patrol in a vehicle, they drive through a neighborhood but do not interact with those on the streets. Not only does this act as less of a deterrent, since the police move quickly through the neighborhood and are less of a presence, but this also results in the police not getting to know the people. If a crime is thus committed, there is less likely to be support and help for the police, and those in the neighborhood are less likely to have a positive feeling toward officers. By choosing foot patrol, the police are forced to interact closely with the people in the neighborhoods and streets they are patrolling.

Horse patrol—the patrolling of beats on horseback—may increase positive community relations, and horses can help officers navigate rugged terrain better than vehicles can. Horse patrol may be a better option than patrolling in cars, since the police will be more visible and approachable and will again be forced to interact with the people where they live, just as they would with foot patrol. Horse patrol may also be superior to foot patrol because, while the police still get the benefits of more community interaction, police who are on horseback can cover more ground than police who are walking patrols on foot.

Beat Boundaries

Beat boundaries are established by trying to create an equal amount of downtime across all beats. Essentially, this means that police are assigned to patrol set areas based on how much action that officer expects to see in a given area. If there is an area of high crime in a police officer's beat, then the officer may also be assigned to a low-crime area as well. This allows his obligations to even out so that a single officer or group of officers is not left with the major crime areas and the largest amount of work while other officers are able to patrol neighborhoods where hardly anything ever happens that requires them to intervene or make reports.

Routine Preventive Patrols

Routine preventive patrols are carried out in beats and districts. This essentially means that the police are given a set area—called their district or beat—that they are supposed to patrol on a regular basis at a regular interval or time. The police then drive (or walk or go on horseback) through this area. There are many purposes to this, including getting to know the people within a neighborhood to foster good community relations. The main and most important purpose, however, is to act as a method of crime prevention. In areas where it is known that the police patrol regularly, individuals may be less likely to commit crimes than in areas where they are aware that there is a limited or nonexistent police presence.

MADD

Mothers Against Drunk Driving (MADD) began as a group of concerned mothers who either feared drunk driving or who had a family member who had been affected by drunk driving. MADD grew to a national organization with a presence in all 50 states, and the organization put immense pressure on legislatures, lobbying for tougher DUI and DWI laws and greater education about the risks and dangers of DWI. MADD also grew to include subsets, such as Students Against Drunk Driving

(SADD), which has the same basic aim as MADD. Today, these organizations continue to lobby for tough laws and for greater education as to the dangers of drunk driving.

Effect of the Civil Rights Movement

In many ways, since many race riots were prompted by police-related activities, the police realized the need to improve their image with the public. Prior to the 1960s there was a great deal of racial discrimination and racial prejudice on the part of the police in certain areas, especially among those in the South, toward African Americans. As people became more sensitive to the rights of minorities, it became incumbent upon the police to act to protect those minorities rather than to act to oppress them.

Police Professionalism

Professionalism in the police is the formalization of a police officer's duties and the corresponding public acceptance of the police force. Professionalism involves doing the job of patrolling, investigating, or whatever other specific duties an officer is assigned, according to the requirements of the law and the purpose of the job. Professionalism involves things such as following the Constitution and the law and never engaging in behavior such as using violence, coercing witnesses, or taking bribes. Essentially, it means that police are held to a high standard of doing their jobs, both so that the community will have greater respect for them and so that they may be more successful at actually enforcing the law.

Professionalism limits inappropriate discretionary activities of an individual employed in the law enforcement field. There are many different examples of what such professionalism may limit. Examples include: the taking of bribes instead of arresting a person for a crime he has committed; the theft of evidence; engaging in illegal searches; coercing a confession; intimidating witnesses; planting evidence or otherwise doing things that would be considered unprofessional and unbecoming conduct for an officer of the law. A police officer who took a monetary bribe or who left the scene of a drug arrest with some of the drugs in his own pocket instead of turning the drugs over as evidence would all considered to be acting unprofessionally.

Law Enforcement Code of Ethics

The Law Enforcement Code of Ethics was developed by Douglass M. Kelley in 1956 to guide the ethics of law enforcement officers. This code set many of the standards of police professionalism and listed both behavior that was desirable as well as behavior that was undesirable and should be avoided by officers of the law. Today, many of these ethical guidelines still apply to police officers. An ethical violation by a police officer will generally be investigated by the Internal Affairs division of the police force and can result in penalties ranging from loss of job to criminal sanctions, depending on the nature of the ethical violation.

Adherence to Moral Obligations and Duties

The special responsibility of a police officer to adhere to moral obligations and duties inherent in police work is referred to as police ethics. Police ethics guide police officers' actions and activities to ensure that they do all tasks in keeping with the spirit of their role. Police officers are considered to be officers of the law and are expected to uphold that law in all people as well as in themselves. An ethical violation could be against the rules and regulations of the police force where a given officer works as well and thus may be more than just a moral violation—violating the duty of ethics could result in an officer being subject to sanctions.

POST

Peace Officer Standards and Training (POST) is the program that all states have put into place to teach and explain ethics to police officers. The purpose is to ensure that police understand the obligations imposed on them. There are some police officials who tend to believe that the end justifies the means and that unethical behavior is OK as long as it is for a good purpose, such as finding and convicting a criminal. The ethics program teaches that the end does not justify the means and that moral and ethical behavior is essential to successful police work.

SUBCULTURE

A subculture is a group of people within a culture that differ somehow from the culture as a whole. A subculture can exist in two forms that relate to law enforcement. First, there can be a subculture within the police force or law enforcement unit. This can involve a subculture of police who are corrupt and undermine the entire system of police and law enforcement. Second, there can be a subculture in the community where a given police force operates. A subculture of violence, for example, may exist in a given community. This can result in a rise in the crime rate as those within the community begin to see violence as an effective means of solving problems. When this occurs, a greater police presence may be required and programs may need to be instituted to change the subculture of violence.

SUBCULTURE OF VIOLENCE

A subculture of violence is a subculture wherein violence is a readily accepted method of resolving conflict. For example, there are certain neighborhoods where gangs become very common. People within those neighborhoods may come to believe that involvement in a gang is normal or accepted, which can lead to further involvement in gangs, which can perpetuate the subculture. When a subculture of violence exists, it becomes more difficult for police to enforce the law because there are many lawbreakers. There may be a need for a larger police presence in the neighborhoods with a subculture of violence in order to break the cycle and to help people to see that violence is not in fact the answer.

SUBCULTURAL THEORY OF CRIMINAL BEHAVIOR

Subcultural theory suggests that group values that support criminal behavior are a significant contributor to criminal activities among certain groups. For example, there are certain communities where drugs are widely accepted. Those within the communities may begin to believe that selling drugs is the only way they can be successful or make a good living, and thus more people may enter the drug subculture. This makes it difficult for law enforcement to stop the behavior, as people don't see selling or using drugs as wrong or as a crime, and instead see it as a normal, accepted way of living. There are many different subcultures that can have a negative impact, such as a subculture of violence in a certain neighborhood where violence becomes the accepted norm.

REACTION FORMATION

Reaction formation refers to the process of a person openly rejecting that to which he or she aspires but feels as though he or she cannot achieve. For example, a person may desire to make an honest living and to get out of a bad neighborhood. However, because of the subculture that exists within that neighborhood and the belief that violence is the accepted answer or that crime is the only way to be successful, the person may reject the idea of "going straight" and making an honest living before he or she even tries it because she believes that making an honest living is impossible.

POLICE SUBCULTURE

A police subculture is the set of attitudes and actions of a police organization that causes the police to identify with one another and differentiates them from the outside world. The most common example of a police subculture is the "blue wall of silence." This is the premise that the police will not testify against each other in the event of corruption because the police need to stick together above all else. A subculture of corruption can also exist wherein a group of police officers begin to accept bribes or otherwise abuse their positions of power. A police subculture can be problematic because it makes it more difficult to enforce the law against police officers or can contribute to increased corruption among officers who might otherwise be honest but who are swayed by the culture of corruption.

The ability to act differently than the rest of the public—the authority to make arrests and use force, for example—contributes to a police subculture. The police may begin to believe that they are above the very laws that they are sworn to uphold and protect. In addition, the fact that police work can be dangerous leads police officers to believe that they must be loyal to each other at all costs and that they must stick together, even if a given officer does not behave ethically or abuses police power.

CODE OF SILENCE

A code of silence means that officers will refuse to testify against one another in instances of misconduct. This is often referred to as the "blue wall of silence." This is a strong negative subculture because it makes it more difficult for police corruption to be stopped and identified. It tends to exist because of the close relationship of police officers who work together and because police officers believe that they are a team together and that they must protect each other at all costs. A subculture involving a code of silence also results in there being resentment, distrust, or dislike of Internal Affairs departments, whose aim it is to identify police corruption.

POLICE CORRUPTION

When a police officer abuses his authority for his own personal gain, it is referred to as police corruption, which comes in many different forms—for example, a police officer checking in evidence at the scene of a crime who slips some of the bills that a drug dealer had in his safe into his own pocket with the belief that no one will miss the money; or an officer accepting a bribe, in cash, goods, or services, in exchange for not making an arrest. If a police officer takes money in order to benefit in exchange for not arresting a suspect, this is obviously police corruption. Police corruption undermines the entire system of law enforcement.

OCCUPATIONAL DEVIANCE

Occupational deviance refers to both criminal and negligent behavior of an officer of the law during a work shift or under the auspices of police authority. Sleeping or intentionally wasting time on the job may both be considered occupational deviance. Other, more serious activities—such as becoming involved in criminal conspiracies, accepting a bribe, or stealing evidence—are generally considered to be more serious than occupational deviance and are classified instead as abuses of power. Occupational deviation also undermines the effectiveness of an officer's ability to do his job to effectively investigate or deter crime. Such instances of occupational deviance are generally handled by the internal affairs department of the police force.

ABUSE OF AUTHORITY

An abuse of authority is significantly more serious than mere "occupational deviance," since abuses of authority often violate inherent rights or harm human dignity. For example, an abuse of authority would involve requiring a person to do something or face arrest. One common example is a police officer who demands free services from a prostitute and threatens that if she does not perform such services, he will place her under arrest. Occupational deviance, on the other hand, is a less serious transgression, such as sleeping on the job instead of patrolling the streets.

Gratuities

Gratuities are free meals or discounts offered to police officers. For example, a police officer might be offered coffee from a restaurant that he attends at no charge. Some departments prohibit police officers from receiving gratuities, while others do not. When gratuities are forbidden by the police force, they are generally prohibited because the force does not want to create an appearance of police corruption or police favoritism. In other forces, the policy against gratuities is not in place because the free items or discounts are usually small items and they are offered by many different businesses that do not hope to gain anything by offering these services to the officers other than to thank the police officers for their work and service at maintaining public safety.

Grass Eaters and Meat Eaters

These terms were thought of for the Knapp Commission and are used to describe the difference between police officers who attempt to refuse or passively accept gratuities (grass eaters) and those who demand them (meat eaters). Grass eaters are generally not considered to be doing anything wrong unless the policy in their district or force forbids them from accepting such gratuities. Those who are meat eaters can be viewed as engaging in an abuse of their power or authority by requiring companies or individuals to give them things they do not deserve.

Bribe

When a police officer is given goods or services in exchange for not enforcing the law, it is referred to as a bribe. There was once a great deal of bribery and corruption rampant in police forces. Today, an increased emphasis on professionalism and police ethics has made it more difficult for police officers to take bribes, and it is more rare for bribery to occur. Unfortunately, bribery still does happen. When it does, it can involve the offer of cash; goods, such as drugs; or services, such as prostitution. No matter what form it takes, bribery undermines the enforcement of the law and gives a bad reputation to police officers, which worsens community relations.

The United States ranks higher than most other countries in terms of police officers' *un*willingness to accept bribes. A part of the reason for this is because bribes are so strongly discouraged within the code of police ethics. Training on police corruption and ethics all emphasize the consequences of bribery and the stringent penalties associated with a corrupt police officer. Internal Affairs departments also act as a strong deterrent to police accepting bribes, as Internal Affairs can effectively investigate and identify many situations where police bribery is occurring.

Pervasive Unorganized Corruption

When there are many different individuals involved in police corruption but those individuals do not work together to organize the corruption, this is referred to as *pervasive unorganized corruption*. Pervasive unorganized corruption can be more difficult than organized corruption to investigate because it may take many different forms. For example, some police officers may accept bribes, while others may take money or drugs that are supposed to be entered into evidence. When pervasive unorganized corruption exists, it can result in crimes in that precinct's area not being prosecuted and can thus create both a rise in the crime rate in a given area and a distrust of the police force in the community where the corruption exists.

Pervasive organized corruption may penetrate into the higher levels of a police department, with most individuals knowingly involved. In other words, if there are several corrupt police officers who join together to create a ring of corruptions and cover-ups, this is considered to be pervasive organized corruption.

This is dangerous because it results in crimes not being prosecuted and in the law not being adequately enforced. Criminals who become aware of the pervasive organized corruption will begin to feel above the law, and the crime rate is likely to go up as word spreads among the criminal element that the police are corrupt and willing to selectively enforce laws. The community may also develop a deep mistrust of police officers as a result of corruption that is occurring.

POLICE DISCRETION

Police discretion is the ability of an officer of the law to make a choice among several possible courses of action. Police discretion is essential to effective police work, because while police must enforce the law, there are sometimes gray areas in law enforcement. For example, police may be willing to overlook a minor offense, such as prostitution, if the individual who is guilty of the minor offense is willing to cooperate in a larger and more serious investigation, such as the investigation of a murder or of organized crime. Police discretion is thus positive and essential, as long as that discretion is not abused.

Police discretion is an important topic because officers of the law must make a wide array of day-to-day choices that the public often might not have to consider. Police officers must always attempt to use their best judgment. Using their discretion effectively to make decisions is essential to successful police work, especially when police must make split-second decisions in life or death situations. Police discretion, however, must be exercised within the bounds of the law. Police officers, for example, have discretion to determine when there are exigent circumstances that allow them to enter an apartment but must not trample on a person's right to privacy as guaranteed by the US Constitution.

Officers of the law must be curious, able to perceive danger, exercise self-control, use varied approaches to crime solving, and possess a tragic (or empathetic) perspective. Almost any time police officers have to make decisions that are not directly governed by the law or the code of police ethics, they must exercise discretion. For example, when police are trying to get a confession to a crime, the officer must decide which questioning tactic will be most likely to encourage the individual to confess: gaining trust, baiting, or using a good cop–bad cop approach.

The seriousness of the offense is the most significant factor affecting police officers' discretion. Officers may, for example, use their discretion to not arrest and prosecute jaywalkers, since arresting these people would be a waste of police resources. With a more serious offense, like DUI, or theft or murder, it no longer becomes appropriate in most cases for police officers to use their discretion to not arrest the individual. Police can also exercise discretion in deciding who should become a confidential informant and be given a lesser sentence in exchange for turning over information on more serious crimes. Often, police discretionary decisions are made after consultation with prosecuting attorneys. Police discretion must also be exercised fairly and without prejudice or bias.

Vice crimes and domestic violence lend themselves most readily to discretionary decisions. Vice crimes lend themselves to discretionary decisions because they are largely victimless crimes—there is no complaining witness or victim in a prostitution case or a gambling case for the most part, and thus no one will be left feeling as though the police did not enforce his or her rights if the police choose not to make an arrest in a vice crime. Domestic violence, as well, lends itself to discretion because often the people who are involved in the domestic violence call are not the ones making a complaint. For example, if the neighbors call the police to a house where a couple is fighting, the couple may not wish to make a complaint and the police officers may have to determine if they believe the victim is in danger of being harmed or not.

Although it is viewed more positively than it once was, police discretion can carry both negative and positive connotations. Police discretion is viewed as a positive because it is necessary to enforce the law and ensure public safety. If police did not have discretion to make decisions, they might be unable to go into an apartment where a crime was taking place because they would be bound by the Constitution. However, they can use discretion to determine that there are exigent circumstances. The negative side of police discretion, however, is that there is always the possibility for discretion to be abused. Police officers may abuse discretion due to a number of biases—race, gender, religion, age, appearance, etc. If a police officer pulls a person over solely on the basis of race, this is an example of misuse of police discretion. Instead of the police officer using unbiased judgment to determine whether to pull that person over, the discretionary decision making of the officer was corrupted by personal prejudice or bias. Police must therefore be trained in police ethics and in the appropriate use of discretion so that it is not abused.

Police discretion is not inherently harmful; rather, inappropriate use (or abuse) of discretion can harm a department's reputation. Some degree of discretion is always required because there are so many decisions that police officers must make on a day-to- day basis that it would be impossible for him to have a clear guide for every decision he must make. If he appropriately makes the decision based on his sworn duty to uphold the law, then his discretion can allow him to better solve crimes, save lives, and otherwise ensure that the community as a whole is properly protected.

Discretion of Prosecutors and Judges

Prosecutors and judges must also exercise discretion. Prosecutors, for example, have a great many decisions to make wherein they must use their best judgment. They must determine whether or not to prosecute a given case and whether they believe a person to be truly innocent or guilty. They must also determine when to arrange a plea bargain with a given offender. Judges, on the other hand, must use their discretion to interpret the law and make decisions on a given case. For example, when judges are asked whether a given piece of information can be entered into evidence, they must use their discretion to interpret evidence law to decide whether the evidence is admissible or not.

Administrative Discretion

"Administrative discretion" refers to the determination of an agency's orientation by its administrator. Administrative discretion is the most important and influential form of police discretion. An administrator might require officers to focus on certain types of crimes, may allocate different numbers of officers to different locations, or determine where to spend the budget of that department. Often, there are too many crimes or locations for police to investigate everything or to be everywhere at once. As such, discretion is necessary to determine where resources are focused in order to ensure the most effective police work and law enforcement. Such discretion must be exercised appropriately, with an eye toward ethics and an unbiased view of the law.

When the head of an entire administrative agency exercises his discretion, it can impact the way all officers under that official act or behave. This can be a positive if the discretion is exercised appropriately, because a positive police subculture can develop wherein the police are working as a unified team to enforce the law. When administrative discretion is exercised inappropriately, it can be a negative because it can create a culture of discrimination or corruption.

Enforcement Discretion

Enforcement discretion is the discretion utilized by officers of the law in determining how to maintain order, enforce the law, and service the public. Enforcement discretion may involve police officials making decisions about which crimes to devote more of their investigative resources to, since not every crime can necessarily be investigated due to the limited number of police officers and of funds. Enforcement discretion is a necessary part of effective police work, but it must be exercised objectively and with an eye toward upholding the law and maintaining police ethics or it can become a detrimental force.

Control over Police Discretion

The courts are the most visible body of external control over police discretion. The courts can control police discretion by setting limits on when police have gone too far. For example, if a police officer behaves in a manner that is not in accordance with his legal duties, the courts can exclude evidence that the officer obtained improperly. This evidence can range from a confession that the courts believe was coerced to the exclusion of evidence found during an illegal search. The police administration will review the officer's decisions and discretionary choices to determine whether those choices fall within the bounds of the law and its requirements in making such decisions.

Legislative Control

The legislative branch may enact laws and provide funds and oversight to direct police discretion one way or another. For example, the legislature may determine that a given area needs to have a larger amount of police present because of rising crime rates. This can result in the hiring of more police within that given area. Legislatures may also create more funding for departments of the police force designed to enforce certain crimes. In addition, in some states, certain behaviors- such as smoking marijuana- have been decriminalized by the legislature, changing the way in which police enforce drug offenses.

Community Policing Model

Community policing seeks to create a collaborative effort between the community and police departments to solve criminal issues—the police are thus both the citizens and the actual law enforcement officials who work together. According to the community policing model, the police and the public are one in the same, with priorities in accordance with one another's. Police and the community work together, in programs such as Neighborhood Watch programs, in order to enforce the legal rules of a given community. This not only acts as a good crime deterrent but also improves relations between the police and the community.

Unlike traditional policing, which focuses on response times, the ultimate goal of community policing is enforcing public cooperation. The success of community policing involves the police and the community in being able to communicate, determine what role each party will play, and facilitate the opportunity for the community to inform police of crimes and help to identify criminals in existence. The idea is to make use of the resources of the community to solve crimes that the individuals who live there may be uniquely aware of and to improve relations between the police and the community.

Traditionally, police officers operated in a community but usually did not live there or interact with the people who did. A community policing model requires police officers to become an integral part of the community they help to serve and protect. Officers get to know the people within the community as they set up community policing endeavors and are able to turn to that community for help in enforcing the law. The community also gets to know the police officers and believe that it has trusted advocates who are working to protect it.

African American Views of Police Officers

According to studies, attitudes toward individual police officers are lower among blacks in the community policing model. Studies showed dissatisfaction with police officers in the model among

African Americans. The reasons for this dissatisfaction are not clear, but indications are that the interaction among the police and African Americans have not always been positive and that true communication and collaboration were not reached. The distrust of police officers that pervades some African American subcultures, as well as the racial prejudice and bias that pervades some police subcultures, could also have contributed to the problems created by community policing methods in African American communities.

Community Consensus of Community Problems

As a general matter, there is usually not a high level of consensus within communities in regard to what those particular problems are or of how to solve them. One of the problems with the community policing model was simply that individuals within a community could not agree upon the goals of the police, or even what their "community" was, leading to confusion. For example, people took different moral attitudes toward vice crimes, drug enforcement, and otherwise "victimless" crimes, and this led to dissatisfaction with the efforts imposed by the community policing method to work together to enforce the laws relating to these crimes.

Goals in Comparison to Traditional Model

The goals of community policing may in fact be in direct opposition to traditional police goals. Many believe that community policing is inefficient, or even a total waste of a department's valuable time and resources. Community policing puts too much discretion into the hands of a community that may not be united, resulting in resources being spread too thin or being squandered, as police do not have a clear idea of where to place their emphasis and focus. In a more traditional model, with administrative and police discretion taking precedence, there can be a uniform decision on what issues and crimes deserve the most attention and resources. Thus, the most pervasive and important problems within a community can be identified and tackled more effectively.

Community Policing Type Activities

Neighborhood Watches, crime education programs, and social service programs run by the government or civic organizations are all aspects of community engagement that do not require a community to necessarily adopt a community policing model. They do not necessarily require the same one-on-one interaction or levels of communication between the police and the community. Neighborhood Watches, for example, can be organized solely by a neighborhood alone, without the partnership or involvement of the police.

Organization of Community

Police officers can provide a community with support and stability, identifying leaders, partnering with religious groups, and helping to build infrastructure. Since communities often do not agree on what issues should be dealt with, who should be in charge, or how things should be resolved, the assistance of police to create broader organization can help create a community environment in which people are actually able to work together toward a more common goal. Police discretion can thus extend down to the community to help it focus on the same important issues that police have identified as being appropriate to allocate resources toward.

Efforts to Fight Crime

Crime reduction need not suffer due to community policing and may in fact improve somewhat due to it. Whether or not community policing is effective or detracts from efforts to fight crime depends on a number of factors, including the amount of consensus within the community, whether or not the community supports the community policing effort, how well organized the police department is and whether its goals align with those of the public, and the types of community policing programs in a given area.

ARRESTS

Making arrests is often viewed as the primary role of police officers by the public. When a police officer makes an arrest, this begins the process of criminal law enforcement. Following an arrest, the person is arraigned and given the opportunity to plead guilty or not guilty. He is then subject to a trial or enters into a plea bargain. Before police can make an arrest, they must be reasonably certain that the individual they are arresting has committed a crime. Sometimes this is simple, such as when they catch a person in the act of breaking the law. At other times, it can involve investigation and collection of evidence to identify the perpetrator who should be arrested.

PREJUDICE

Prejudice is a reflection of one's values, positive or negative, that develop as a result of the socialization process. It causes individuals to "prejudge" one another on the basis of numerous deep-seated ideas about groups of people. There are many examples of prejudices. People may be prejudiced against a given gender or against a certain race or nationality of people. Racial profiling stems from the concept of prejudice. When a police officer is prejudiced, it can affect his discretionary decision making and can interfere with his ability to enforce the law in the fair and unbiased manner that is required of him as an officer of the law.

DISCRIMINATION

Discrimination occurs when an individual acts solely on the basis of his or her prejudices for or against a group of people. Prejudice, by itself, is simply the act of prejudging a person based on certain characteristics, such as race and gender. Prejudice itself is a negative characteristic, since it is not legal or morally right to prejudge a person. However, when prejudice actually becomes discrimination when an officer acts on that prejudice, the problem becomes much more serious. Discrimination can interfere with police officers' ability to do their job appropriately. It can also result in the community developing a negative view of the police as a result of the idea that the police are prejudiced against a given minority group.

OFFENDER VARIABLES

Offender variables are an offender's age, race, demeanor, and socioeconomic status. In most cases, consideration of these offender variables in determining how a person is to be treated is inappropriate—but not always. For example, a police officer choosing to arrest one person because he is African American while letting a Caucasian go for the same offense would be an example of a misuse of offender variables. Deciding that a person should be questioned because he has a suspicious demeanor may be an appropriate use of offender variables. Police discretion can come into play when considering offender variables, but it must be exercised in an unbiased and fair manner.

SITUATIONAL VARIABLES

The presence of others, the visibility of an officer's actions, and the danger of a situation are all examples of *situational variables*. For example, a police officer may decide to let a drunk person off with a warning if that person is alone in his apartment hallway and is sleeping, but he might arrest that same person for public intoxication if the person is sleeping out in public, where he creates a disturbance. A police officer may also decide to apprehend a criminal he believes is armed if that criminal is alone but he may decide to wait and/or follow the person to a quieter area if the armed suspect is in a crowd of innocent bystanders who could be hurt if the armed suspect pulled a gun.

SYSTEM VARIABLES

Officers' perception of the law, relationships with peers, and attitudes of the community are all considered *system variables*. For example, police officers who are in subcultures of being tough on crime may be more eager to make arrests for minor violations for which, outside of that culture, they would have let the violators off with a warning. Police officers may also use their discretion to enforce laws against public drunkenness more in communities that are strongly against such displays of intoxication than in larger cities, where it is more accepted for there to be drunk, homeless people on the street.

TREATMENT OF AFRICAN AMERICANS VS. CAUCASIANS

Studies have demonstrated that, for whatever reason, blacks are treated more harshly. However, reasons vary as to why this might be the case. While racism is often the answer given, other factors, such as racial composition of the location, may also be to blame. Racism and police prejudice are, unfortunately, still in existence despite efforts to eradicate them through police professionalism and ethics codes that prohibit racial profiling. This can create public relations problems for the police and adversely affect police departments' reputation and standing within given communities.

DOMESTIC VIOLENCE

Domestic violence refers to an incident that results in physical harm, or the threat of physical harm, by one member of a household to another. Domestic violence is commonly thought of as being perpetrated by a husband against his wife or female partner. However, domestic violence is not limited to such situations. In fact, domestic violence by women against men is becoming recognized as more of a problem. Domestic violence can also occur between gay and lesbian couples, or even between those who are not in a romantic relationship at all, such as roommate situations or between family members who share a home.

Attitudes toward domestic violence have changed. Policing has changed along with the culture. While what occurred in the home was once viewed as the private affair of those individuals, and victims were seen as being unwilling to seek help, today domestic violence often results in arrests. This has come in part because of an increased focus on women's rights, since women are no longer viewed as being the property of their husbands. In addition, there is increased recognition that domestic violence is not always by a man against a woman, but may also be by a woman against her male partner.

VICE CRIMES

Vice crimes—crimes against public order or morality, such as prostitution and gambling—are seen by some as being "victimless," while others contend that vice crimes do cause actual physical and/or spiritual harm. Those who believe that the crimes are victimless argue that prostitutes and gambling do not actually hurt anyone, while those who believe that the crimes cause harm cite many different reasons, ranging from the negative effect of the so-called victimless crimes on the communities to the fact that prostitution or gambling can lead to other, more serious, and violent crimes, such as violence by pimps against prostitutes or theft resulting from a need to pay gambling debts.

ARRESTS

Vice laws constitute a comparatively small portion of arrests. This, in part, could be due to selective enforcement of vice laws by police departments that allocate their resources toward enforcing more serious and violent crimes. This could also be due to the fact that since there is no "victim," many of the vice crimes go unreported. For example, unless police patrol an area and catch a prostitute in the act, neither the prostitute nor the person employing his or her services is going to come forward and report the illegal action to the police department.

Prostitution

People engaged in prostitution are often at a high risk for disease and violence. The spread of communicable diseases such as HIV and AIDS can also occur as a result of prostitution and can spread to the mainstream community if a person who uses a prostitute then engages in consensual sex with other individuals. There is a subculture among prostitution where violence is largely accepted by pimps against prostitutes, and there is also a market for prostitutes who are willing to allow people to engage in sexual behavior without wearing a condom, often for an additional fee. Many believe that those involved in prostitution are often victims themselves, such as young runaways from abusive home situations.

Problems with Pornography

Individuals may be against pornography for a number of reasons. Feminists often argue that pornography is degrading to women. They believe that it promotes violence toward and objectification of women. It is also argued that it objectifies women and can cause women to suffer lowered self-esteem. Many also argue that those who become involved in the pornography industry are often victims, subject to abuse or other problems that led them to become involved in the industry in the first place. Finally, those engaged in the process of making pornography typically have multiple partners, which is high-risk sexual behavior that can increase the spread of sexually transmitted diseases.

Connection to Violent Sex Offenses

According to studies, pornography does not correlate with violent sex offenses. While arguments can and are made that pornography encourages violence against women or a misogynistic attitude toward women that leads to more violent sex offenses, the scientific studies done to date do not support this theory. Even violent pornography, such as that glorifying rape or other depravities against women, does not necessarily inspire more violent sex crimes, although there are those who argue passionately that it does. There simply is no conclusive evidence to suggest this correlation.

Views of Gambling

While gambling was once tied to organized crime, in this day and age many departments choose to ignore gambling altogether and focus on larger crimes. While there is still some degree of bookmaking and organized crime involvement in gambling, legalized gambling on Indian reservations and in Las Vegas, Reno, and Atlantic City has lessened the need for the large-scale dangerous gambling rings that were once run by organized crime. Small-scale gambling operations, such as poker clubs, have also become more accepted, as poker has become a part of popular culture. And as community attitudes have changed, so too have police attitudes toward enforcing anti-gambling laws.

Strategic Policing

Strategic policing is a model that enlarges the enforcement target of law enforcement officials to include nontraditional offenders such as white collar criminals, drug distribution rings, and serial offenders. These crimes were traditionally under-investigated due to the fact that there do not tend to be complaining victims for certain white collar crimes, as well as the fact that cover-ups are rampant and that identifying crimes and investigating crimes tend to be much more complex. However, efforts such as the use of undercover officers have helped to make it more possible to investigate these specific areas of crime.

Female Police Officers

Often, female police officers do not share the same interests as their male counterparts. Female police officers have altered the traditionally "masculine" vibe of policing. Female police officers may attempt to understand what occurred at a more personal and human level, rather than purely from the level of gathering information and evidence. For example, a woman police officer may take a different approach to interviewing a witness, using more listening and empathy than straight questioning. Female police officers may also focus their investigation more on identifying the motives of a given crime and getting inside the head of the criminal who perpetrated it. Studies have shown that female officers issue slightly fewer citations and make slightly fewer arrests but that they are not as likely as males to engage in activities considered "unbecoming" of a police officer.

Excessive Force

Views differ as to whether females or males are more likely to use excessive force. While women may be slightly less likely to use excessive force, studies have also demonstrated that female and male police officers perform their duties remarkably similarly, making this disparity seem insignificant. The slight disparity could also be explained by suspects not wishing to make reports of force being used on them by a woman, especially if the suspect is male and they do not want to be made to seem as if a woman was able to overpower them.

Attitudes Toward Female Police Officers

Attitudes toward women in the service have changed quite a bit, with men gradually coming to accept the role of policewomen over time. Initially, there was a stereotype that police work was too dangerous and/or too physical for women and that women would not be able to apprehend larger suspects or act as a sufficient crime deterrent. With more and more women becoming a part of the police force, these stereotypes have changed and women have become largely accepted, although there are still subsets of officers who have a difficult time with the concept.

The three types of views that male police officers may adopt of female law enforcement officials are traditional, modern, and moderate. Traditionals have the most difficulty accepting the role of females in the police force. Moderates often don't like women on patrol duty, but support them in uniform, while moderns are not tied to traditional views of women's roles in uniform and tend to be the most accepting. Overall, however, the willingness to accept women on the police force has changed over the years as women's rights issues have come more to the forefront and it has become more normal to see female police officers.

Recent Trends

While originally the numbers of female police officers climbed, it seems to have leveled off at a "glass ceiling" of around 13 to 14 percent of hires, and the number of females in supervisory roles to this day remains rather low. This could be due to many factors, including the fact that more men than women are interested in working in the police force. Another contributing factor is that women tend to be more likely to leave the force to raise children than men do. The specific reasons why this trend is occurring have not been identified, but efforts are made to encourage the hiring and promotion of female police officers where possible.

Support of Change in Police Departments

African American law enforcement officials generally feel more comfortable with change than white ones, according to many studies. This result could, in part, be due to the fact that positions of power on the police force are no longer strictly for white males, and thus there is a subculture of those who feel threatened by the potential shift away from the traditional power structures and roles. However, the results are not conclusive as to why Caucasian officers are more resistant to change.

Effect of Race on Performance

There is little evidence to suggest that race or ethnicity affect an officer's performance. Caucasian officers may be more likely to exhibit discretionary bias against minorities and to use tactics like racial profiling. However, there is no conclusive evidence to prove that one race is any more or less effective or performs police work in any substantially different ways.

Education Level of Police Officers

The education levels of police officers have risen significantly and steadily over time. This is in large part due to police departments imposing more requirements to qualify for the police academy. As a general matter, most police academies require no less than a high school diploma and many require additional schooling in the form of either an associates or a bachelor's degree before an individual will be admitted as a recruit to the police academy. The increased education level is widely seen as a good thing.

Representation of Minorities

While racial minorities are approaching their levels of representation in communities throughout the country, women remain significantly underrepresented in most police departments in the United States. It has become more widely accepted for females to be on the police force and yet this number does remain small. There is some speculation as to the reason for the relatively small number of women, including the danger of the job and the high demands of time and energy. These things contribute to the fact that women may tend to leave the job more often when they have families than men do, as it is difficult to balance being a mother with a job without regular hours and where there is such high risk.

Female and Male Ability to Defuse Potentially Violent Confrontations

Female police officers, according to studies, often excel in such situations. There are a number of potential reasons why this may be the case. Women may be better at listening and openly communicating with the person who has a tendency to be violent. They may be able to intuitively understand how to diffuse a situation and how to use reasoning skills with the potential violent offender. Male officers may tend to take a more traditional or hardnosed approach to the negotiations, which can detract from their effectiveness and can result in violence escalating rather than diffusing the situation.

Learning Organization

A "learning organization" seeks to acquire the knowledge to modify its behavior and insights—the ability to adapt. In other words, learning organizations are more willing to identify what is and is not working through introspective self-study and make changes. Some police forces are more interested in becoming learning organizations, which tends to make them more effective, while there are subcultures of police and law enforcement that are more resistant to change and more focused on keeping the policies and procedures the same as they always were, regardless of whether those methods are the most effective or not.

Affirmative Action

Because of the disparity of minorities in police management, affirmative action has sought to place more minorities into higher-level positions in police departments and organizations. This can be beneficial in many ways, such as bringing broader perspectives and underrepresented groups into the law enforcement world. Since women tend to be more effective at diffusing violent situations, this can be viewed as a positive thing. Further, studies suggest that minorities and nonminorities are equally effective at police work and law enforcement activities. Affirmative action may also help to cut down on racial profiling, not only because there are more minorities but also because police officers will have to work with minorities and examine their own prejudices.

United States Law and Precedent

Supreme Law of the Land

The US Constitution is the highest law in the land. Any law that is passed must be in accordance with the Constitution and its aims. If the legislature passes a law that conflicts with the Constitution, the law can be challenged by an individual who is directly affected by it and the court can determine that the law is unconstitutional and thus void. Police officers, as well, must follow the Constitution in doing their jobs and must ensure that they respect any and all constitutional rights of a person they may be investigating. However, the Constitution may be changed or added to with the addition of amendments.

Bill of Rights

The first ten amendments are commonly referred to as the Bill of Rights. These were written shortly after the passing of the Constitution. These include the right to freedom of speech and the press, the right to bear arms, the right not to incriminate oneself or be subject to search and seizure without probable cause, the right to due process, the right to a fair trial by jury, the right not to be subject to cruel and unusual punishment, and the right to life, liberty, and the pursuit of happiness. These first ten amendments have been subject to extensive scrutiny and controversy over the years, especially the right to bear arms and how far to extend the right of freedom of speech.

Landmark Court Case

A landmark court case substantially changes the way day-to-day operations of the justice system work and establishes a legal precedent in due process from that point forward. For example, *Miranda v. Arizona* was a landmark case, as it required police officers to read people their rights before any questioning as a suspect or at the time of arrest. Other landmark cases are *Roe v. Wade,* which made abortion legal, and various civil rights cases, such as those that ended segregation.

Miranda v. Arizona

Miranda v. Arizona is a Supreme Court decision made to ensure that those accused of a crime have their constitutional rights respected by law enforcement officials. The decision in *Miranda v. Arizona* resulted in the necessity for police to advise suspects of their rights before they interrogate a suspect—or to read them their "Miranda rights." These rights include the right to remain silent, the right to have an attorney present during questioning, and the right to have an attorney provided if the suspect cannot afford one. The aim of reading an accused criminal his Miranda rights is to make sure he knows of the constitutional protections afforded him, such as the Fifth Amendment right against self-incrimination.

Illegally Seized Evidence

Evidence is described as having been illegally seized when it is taken from a location without the proper search warrant or as the result of interrogations that were conducted unfairly or improperly. For example, if police pull a driver over and search his vehicle without having probable cause to do so, then anything that is turned up is illegally seized evidence. In order for evidence to be considered illegally seized, there must be a right of privacy; in other words, the person must have had the expectation that the item was his private item. Items thrown in the public trash would not be considered illegally seized evidence because there is no expectation of privacy.

Exclusionary Rule

Weeks vs. US established the "exclusionary rule," or the understanding that incriminating evidence must be seized according to the constitutional understanding of the right to due process; otherwise, such evidence may not be used in a court case. This means that any evidence that is admissible in court must have been obtained through proper channels, such as a police officer's first showing probable cause and getting a search warrant. If a police officer entered someone's home without permission to search for evidence, then the person's expectation of privacy and constitutional right against search and seizure would be violated and the evidence would not be admissible.

Good Faith Exception

There may be exceptions to the exclusionary rule on "good faith"—for example, officers who make an honest mistake in obtaining evidence may still be permitted to use that evidence in court because the officers did not willfully violate a person's constitutional rights and because, since there was no willful violation, it is in the interests of justice to permit the evidence to be admitted in court.

Legally Obtained Evidence

The 1960s case *Mapp v. Ohio* established the rule that evidence obtained in violation of the fourth amendment's "unreasonable searches and seizures" clause may not be used in a court of law. If evidence that was illegally seized were able to be used in court, this would undermine the Constitution's purpose in protecting the right to privacy, since there would be no deterrent to police from illegal searching to obtain evidence. Because the evidence may not be used unless it is obtained through proper channels, police are more careful to ensure that they follow the rules of evidence and the proper procedures when investigating a crime, thus ensuring due process to every accused person.

Exceptions

The exclusionary rule requires that all evidence be obtained legally, within a person's constitutional rights. Evidence that is not obtained legally is not admitted in court. To legally obtain evidence, police generally must have probable cause and a search warrant in order to search homes and obtain evidence. However, some exceptions exist to this rule, including stop and frisk, good faith seizure of evidence, seizure of evidence in plain view, arrest based on computer error, and authority to enter an open field without a warrant, among others. This means that police can stop people and frisk them to find weapons—and if anything else illegal is found, it is admissible. The same is true if the police pull a driver over and see drugs on the seat next to the person—this is in plain view and the evidence can thus be seized.

In Plain View

An object is considered to be in plain view when it is readily visible to an officer who has a legal right to be in the viewing area and who has reason to believe that the evidence was involved in or associated with criminal activity. For example, if police pull a driver over for a broken tail light and see drugs or alcohol in plain view on the front seat, this can be considered to be in plain view, and the evidence can be seized by the police. However, drugs inside of a closed glove compartment would not fall within the "plain view" doctrine and the police would not be able to use evidence they found inside the glove compartment unless they either had permission to search it or had a search warrant to do so.

Most evidence under the plain view doctrine is discovered inadvertently or accidentally, although this condition is not necessary for an officer to confiscate evidence under its authority. For example, if a police officer pulls a driver over and happens to see something illegal in the car, this is an accidental discovery of the evidence found under the "in plain view" doctrine. However, if the police suspected a person stole a necklace, rang a doorbell to talk to that person, and the person was wearing the necklace, this might not be considered "accidental" discovery, but it can still be considered to fall under the plain view exception.

The "in plain view" doctrine does not change even when the police officer is invited into a home. Those invited into a home must act as guests, not interrogators, thus even a suspect has a reasonable expectation to privacy. For example, if a person invites a police officer into a house and the police officer asks to go to the bathroom, and while in there he opens the person's medicine cabinet to find evidence of drugs, then this would not be considered to be within the plain view doctrine, since it is not normal guest behavior to open a person's medicine cabinet. This would be considered an illegal search and the drugs found in the medicine cabinet would not be considered admissible in court.

Wolf v. Colorado

Contrary to what the law would later determine, this court case held that the 14th Amendment to the Constitution did not specifically limit criminal justice and that "illegally seized" evidence could be admitted into a court case. However, this decision was later overturned when the US Supreme Court more carefully considered the purpose and intent of constitutional rights and determined that a person's rights to privacy and against unlawful search and seizure were not fully respected if the police could simply illegally search and have the evidence admitted anyway.

Searching a Home After an Arrest

According to *Chimel v. California*, police may search the entire home after an arrest only if a warrant is first obtained. An arrest, of course, is not a conviction, and people must still have all of their due process rights respected. Thus, as in any situation where they want to search, the police must show probable cause to a judge who signs a warrant permitting that search. Failure to obtain a proper warrant can result in any evidence identified during the search being considered inadmissible in a court of law.

Search of Surrounding Areas

The defendant and the immediate surrounding area within the defendant's reach may be searched if an individual is apprehended. Officers may conduct a search to protect themselves (i.e., to identify whether a person is carrying any weapons). The police are also allowed to conduct this search to prevent evidence from being destroyed and to prevent the offending individual from fleeing the scene. However, the police may not search other surrounding areas, such as the person's home, even if the person has been arrested, without the proper warrant to do so.

Exigent Circumstances Search

In certain emergencies, such as when human life or the destruction of evidence is at stake, an emergency search conducted by the police without a warrant may result in the discovery of evidence that may be used in a court of law. For example, if a police are walking down the street and hear a woman screaming inside of an apartment, the police can enter that apartment without an invitation or a search warrant as long as they reasonably believe that the person inside of the apartment is in danger. If the police see evidence of a crime after they have entered to save the screaming women, then the police may take that evidence and use it in court, even if they did not have a search warrant to enter. This situation is also called an exigent circumstances search. *Warden v. Hayden* in 1967 first approved the warrantless search of evidence after reports that an armed robber had fled into the building.

Emergency Search of an Individual

In situations that are dire and require immediate action, such as an individual matching the description of an armed suspect or a man being found unresponsive in a park, a search of an individual may be conducted. The police must reasonably believe that there is imminent danger, and if any evidence is uncovered, the police will generally have to justify their actions in searching the individual in order for that evidence to be admitted in court. In this way, the courts ensure that a person's constitutional rights are respected but that those rights are weighed against the importance of public safety.

Search of Impounded Vehicles

A car that is impounded is taken by a tow truck to a police impound yard, based on some violation such as being parked in a tow away zone or belonging to a person who has a series of unpaid traffic tickets. A vehicle that is impounded may be searched if the search is undertaken for routine and reasonable purposes, such as the safekeeping and inventorying of an individual's property. The vehicle, of course, must have been impounded for a legitimate reason, i.e., for some violation of the law that a car would normally be impounded for, in order for the search to be legal or the evidence obtained to be admissible in court.

Fleeing-Targets Exception

Under the fleeing-targets exception to the rule, a warrantless search of a vehicle is permitted. The fleeing-targets exception allows the search of a motor vehicle by law enforcement personnel whose objective is to prevent a vehicle from fleeing the jurisdiction of a particular law enforcement agency. However, the police must have a legitimate reason to believe that the driver of the vehicle is in the process of or intends to flee the jurisdiction. Otherwise, a warrantless search is not generally permitted unless there are exigent circumstances (i.e., the police believe someone is in danger) or there is probable cause (such as an open bottle of alcohol sitting out).

Suspicionless Searches

Under certain circumstances, suspicionless searches can occur when a person is not suspected of criminal activity. Suspicionless searches are allowed only when the search is conducted on the basis on an overriding need to protect the welfare of the public. For example, if a bomb threat has been called in to a particular building, the police may stop and search anyone entering that building to determine whether that person is the one with the bomb. In such a situation, the public interest in conducting the search must be stronger than the public interest in protecting the constitutional rights of the individual(s) subject to the suspicionless search. Random DUI checkpoints are another example of suspicionless search, since every driver—whether exhibiting behavior of drunk driving or not—can be pulled over and examined for evidence of drunkenness at the checkpoint.

Fruit of the Poisoned Tree

This term refers to a principle that excludes any evidence that later develops as a result of illegal search and seizure to be permitted as evidence in the court of law. For example, if police find a key to a storage locker during an illegal search, then the police may not use any evidence they found in that storage locker in a court. Likewise, if the police illegally coerce a confession out of a suspect or if they get a confession without informing a suspect of his rights, then any evidence acquired from that confession (including the location of a dead body) will not be admitted in a court of law. Police must thus be especially carefully of ensuring they do not violate any constitutional rights in investigated crimes, otherwise a guilty person could go free.

Right to Counsel

Escobedo v. Illinois established the right to counsel. In other words, this case established that part of the constitutional right to due process and a fair trial meant that a person had a right to an attorney. Since not everyone can afford an attorney, an attorney must sometimes be provided at the court's expense. This court-appointed counselor, or public defender, helps to ensure that the accused individual has a fair trial and that all of his constitutional rights are safeguarded. Without the right to an attorney, the rights to due process and a fair trial would be hollow, since it is often too difficult for people to navigate through the court system on their own.

Writ of Certiorari

A writ of certiorari is issued by an appellate court to get the record of a case's proceedings from a lower court. When a person is involved in a court case, that person has the right to appeal a decision (with the exception of a prosecutor who loses a criminal case, since the Constitution prohibits double jeopardy, or retrying a person for the same criminal act). The higher court, called an appellate court, must review the record of the lower court to determine whether any legal errors occurred. The court does not review the decisions on facts, but only on the law. Still, it must read the entire record.

Freedom of the Guilty

Unfortunately, police who are not careful enough may violate due process laws, allowing the guilty to go free. The criminal justice situation is constantly changing in the United States, and police officers are charged with the responsibility of carrying out the process as painstakingly as possible to achieve justice. The view, however, of the US criminal justice system is that constitutional rights are inalienable and cannot be violated even for the greater good, otherwise a slippery slope would be created and rights would mean nothing at all. It is also the view of the criminal justice system in the US that it is better for guilty men to go free than for innocent men to be imprisoned, so the rules designed to ensure a fair trial are given the utmost respect and are always enforced—even if it means a guilty man walks free due to procedural violations.

Dollree Mapp

Dollree Mapp was accused of harboring a fugitive wanted in a bombing. It was effectively argued that her home was illegally searched and evidence illegally seized, making her case one of the most important precedent-setting cases of its time. The evidence of her harboring a fugitive was not admitted because of the illegal search. This helped to drive home the point that police must always be careful in exercising discretion and search only with the proper warrant or in exigent circumstances where they truly believed that an imminent and immediate danger existed had they not entered the building at that time.

Conservatism in the Supreme Court

In the 1980s and the early 1990s, due to the influence of Republicans such as Ronald Reagan and George H.W. Bush, the Supreme Court began swinging toward conservatism. The Supreme Court officials are elected by the President when one of the nine seats on the court opens up due to a judge passing away or otherwise becoming unable to serve in the judicial role and thus steps down. Much attention is paid to an election of a President when it is expected that the President will be appointing a Supreme Court justice, because these justices are appointed for life. The makeup of the Court, as far as whether it is conservative or liberal, is very important to the public, since the Court may be asked to make decisions on key issues such as abortion or gay marriage.

PROBABLE CAUSE

Probable cause is a set of facts and circumstances that would cause an average person to determine reasonably that a person had intentionally committed a crime—for example, a police officer seeing a person fleeing from a store where he knows a robbery has just taken place. Probable cause can also exist if a person is found carrying stolen merchandise or with blood on his or her clothes. When probable cause exists, the police can present the probable cause to the prosecutor, who can get a warrant from a judge. Probable cause can also be required to issue an arrest warrant that allows for a person to be arrested in conjunction with a particular crime.

ARREST

An arrest is the taking of an individual into custody for the purpose of charging the person with a criminal offense (or charging a minor with a status offense). An arrest may be done only with probable cause, and generally (but not always) after an arrest warrant has been issued. In general, there are few situations where a police officer can arrest a person unless there has been an investigation and probable cause has been identified or unless the police have witnessed a person in the act of committing a crime. However, community interests may require a suspension of personal rights in the absence of probable cause (such as in instances of drunken driving). This means that if a person is pulled over for drunk driving, the police can automatically arrest and detain him to be taken to the station for further testing (like a blood test).

Police may arrest an individual who is in the process of committing a crime, or a person they believe committed a crime based on evidence. After the arrest, the person has the right to a speedy trial and is generally arraigned first, potentially released on bail, and then tried in a court of law to determine guilt or innocence of the charges.

MIRANDA WARNING

An arrest exists technically when a police officer restricts an individual's freedom to leave a particular area, so a Miranda warning is not necessary in every arrest. However, if the police intend to question a suspect or to gather and collect evidence through speaking to that suspect, then the Miranda warning is generally required. The purpose of this is to ensure that people arresting for committing crimes are aware of their rights and do not have their constitutional protections violated by the police. Failure to read a Miranda warning when required results in evidence being inadmissible in court, so police generally do read people their Miranda rights in any situation of arrest, even if not required to do so.

SEARCH INCIDENT TO ARREST

A search incident to arrest is a warrantless search of an individual who has been arrested, in order to ensure the safety of the arresting officer. This rule was established primarily because the arrested individual may possess weapons. The rule can also be used to ensure that the person does not destroy evidence of the crime. However, search incident to arrest is limited only to searching the person's body and the immediately surrounding area. It is not permissible to search a person's entire home simply because that person has been subject to arrest. To do so, the police would have to get a search warrant.

REASONABLE SUSPICION

Reasonable suspicion is the level of suspicion required to cause an officer to be justified in further inquiry and investigation. In other words, police may not simply investigate or search people—to do so would be a violation of their constitutional right to privacy. There must be some reason to put people under investigation. Examples include eyewitness report of a crime, observing suspicious or potentially illegal behavior, a record of committing crime with a consistent modus operandi, or something else that would lead a reasonable person to believe that the individual in question should be further investigated.

Investigatory Stop

Stops by the police to investigate a person are permissible when they are supported by reasonable suspicion. For example, if a police officer notices an individual swerving or driving erratically, the police may pull the person over to conduct testing to see whether the individual is guilty of driving drunk or driving under the influence. The limits of the investigation are set by what is reasonable, however. In other words, it is not reasonable to assume that a person with a broken tail light is driving drunk, so if the police pull a person over for a broken tail light, the officers may not investigate that person for drunk driving or issue a Breathalyzer test unless the person exhibits other signs of drunkenness after being pulled over for the unrelated reason.

Compelling Interest

A compelling interest is a legal concept providing the basis for a warrant without suspicion when the public welfare may be in jeopardy. If a person is believed to be about to enter a building with a bomb in his vehicle, for example, and there is strong evidence to suggest that there really is a bomb in the car, the police may be able to immediately act to pull the person over and search the car for the bomb—even if they do not have a proper search warrant. Such a search is appropriate only if the public interest is strong enough to override the personal rights to privacy of the individual who is subject to the search.

Inherent Coercion

Inherent coercion involves tactics used by police officers to extract information that fall somewhat short of physical abuse but nevertheless "force" the suspects to divulge information. For example, if a police officer intimidates a person and makes him believe he is going to be in danger, then this could be inherent coercion even if the police never touched the person. Keeping the person in a cold interrogation room for hours without permitting him food, drink, or the opportunity to use the bathroom could be inherent coercion. Essentially, any cruel tactic employed to make a person confess is considered to be inherent coercion.

Psychological Manipulation

Individuals need not be physically coerced in order for the extraction of information to be considered unlawful—psychological manipulation, designed to coerce suspects to divulge information through intimidation or control, was banned in 1954. An example of psychological manipulation is the taking of extremely religious people to a church and urging them to confess their sins, while the police officer stands next to him listening to those sins and using the information obtained as a confession. When psychological manipulation is used, the evidence obtained and the confession itself will not be admissible in court.

Waiving Miranda Rights

The Miranda rights must be read to people who are being questioned by the police as official suspects in order to ensure that the individuals are aware of their rights afforded by the Constitution. If the Miranda rights are not read, anything said in the process of questioning is not admissible. A knowing and intelligent waiver, however, may allow people to legally waive their rights, although to do so is rarely advisable. This means that if the police read people their Miranda rights and they choose to talk without a lawyer present, thus waiving their right to remain silent or have counsel, the information they divulge can be used against them provided their waiver of rights was informed.

DSST Practice Test

1. The world's first modern police force, the Metropolitan Police, was established in the early 19th century in what city?

a. Paris
b. London
c. Stockholm
d. New York City

2. The Metropolitan Police resembled modern police forces in all of the following ways EXCEPT:

a. They wore uniforms to stand out from the public.
b. They patrolled the streets to deter crime.
c. They used military-style hierarchies and administration.
d. They received professional training at an academy.

3. The education advocated by August Vollmer and implemented in criminal justice courses at the University of California in the 1920s could be best characterized as

a. heavily influenced by social-science research.
b. strongly based on criminology.
c. mostly practical training on the administration of police work.
d. derivative of earlier criminal justice education.

4. The Kansas City experiment of the early 1970s provided which of the following results about police patrolling?

a. Increased patrolling reduced preventable crimes.
b. Increased patrolling increased preventable crimes.
c. Decreased patrolling increased preventable crimes.
d. Changes in the amount of patrolling had no significant effect on preventable crimes.

5. The Wickersham Commission of 1931 recognized that Prohibition was unenforceable largely because of an increase in which police activity?

a. Regular police beats disappeared due to the need to enforce Prohibition.
b. Police corruption increased due to the wealth of bootleggers.
c. Border patrols were insufficient at slowing smuggling from Canada.
d. Police were forced to work second jobs due to the Great Depression.

6. The law enforcement of the American frontier until the 19th century could best be characterized as

a. vigilantism.
b. night watch.
c. comes stabuli.
d. directed patrol.

7. Which of the following trial steps is conducted at an initial hearing before a magistrate or lower-court judge?

a. Jury selection begins.
b. Presentation of evidence starts.
c. Consideration of pretrial release.
d. A decision on whether to indict the defendant.

8. Criminal trials in the United States are held under which of the following systems?

a. inquisitorial
b. adversarial
c. judicial
d. procedural

9. Which of the following actions would constitute "preserving the peace" as it applies to the mission of the police?

a. ticketing a man for public urination outside of a bar
b. apprehending a man fleeing the scene of a store robbery
c. investigating a homicide committed in a federal building
d. an officer testifying at the sentencing hearing of a convicted felon

10. Strategic policing would best be used to target which kind of crime?

a. a drug distribution network
b. graffiti on public transportation
c. a holdup outside of an ATM
d. domestic violence

11. Which of the following sentences falls under the rubric of community corrections?

a. A defendant's sentence is commuted due to overcrowding in the prison system.
b. The death penalty is the ultimate sentence available to the federal government and thirty-four states.
c. Victim-impact statements may be used during sentencing in all fifty states.
d. Some states require sex offenders to wear electronic tracking devices.

12. Under which prison classification level are inmates allowed furlough for work or educational purposes?

a. maximum security
b. medium security
c. minimum security
d. shock incarceration

13. How does a nolo contendere plea differ from a guilty plea?

a. There is no difference between the two pleas.
b. The plea cannot be used against the defendant in a civil action.
c. It shows the defendant's refusal to speak.
d. It is only used in plea-bargaining after the arraignment.

14. During jury selection, what kind of challenge to a potential juror can a defense attorney make without giving a reason?

a. challenge to the array
b. challenge for cause
c. peremptory challenge
d. voir dire

15. Which of the following crimes skewed the crime index and caused the reevaluation of Part I offenses in recent years?

a. larceny-theft
b. forcible rape
c. aggravated assault
d. murder

16. What must happen for a crime to be considered "cleared" for the clearance rate portion of UCR/NIBRS statistics?

a. A judge or jury must rule.
b. An arrest must be made.
c. A crime must be reported.
d. An investigation must begin.

17. Which of the following is NOT a federal agency?

a. air marshals
b. highway patrol
c. Secret Service
d. Bureau of Alcohol, Tobacco, Firearms, and Explosives

18. Which of the following crimes falls under the purview of the Federal Bureau of Investigation?

a. domestic violence
b. statutory rape
c. vandalism
d. bribery

19. What characterizes a decentralized model of state law enforcement?

a. Highway patrol officers perform criminal investigations.
b. Highway patrol officers report to federal, state, and local agencies.
c. Highway enforcement is a separate state agency from other law enforcement.
d. Highway enforcement is handled by many separate agencies.

20. Which was the first state to create its own law enforcement agency?

a. Texas
b. Massachusetts
c. Pennsylvania
d. California

21. The title sheriff refers to a law enforcement officer responsible for patrol in which area?

a. incorporated municipalities
b. state highways
c. unincorporated areas of a county
d. cities with populations smaller than 500,000

22. Which of the following levels of law enforcement has grown the most rapidly in the last decade?

a. federal
b. state
c. local
d. private

23. Which of the following reasons is NOT a valid pretext for police to search an area during an arrest without a search warrant?

a. to protect the arresting officers
b. to prevent evidence from being destroyed
c. to keep the defendant from escaping
d. to gather evidence for prosecution

24. Which of the following is inappropriate law enforcement that actually causes a crime to be committed?

a. anomie
b. entrapment
c. collateral estoppel
d. actus reus

25. Which policing style described by James Q. Wilson is characterized by the maintenance of order through selective police intervention?

a. the watchman style
b. the legalistic style
c. the service style
d. the reform style

26. A Bivens action is a lawsuit brought against officers at which level of law enforcement?

a. private security
b. local
c. state
d. federal

27. Which of the following positions in a police department performs duties that would be considered mostly line operations?

a. budget coordinator
b. detective sergeant
c. towing manager
d. media relations

28. Which of the following agencies has jurisdiction to investigate police officers accused of violating a citizen's civil rights?

a. US DEA
b. US DOJ
c. Metropolitan Internal Affairs
d. Secret Service

29. Local police are most likely to use which of the following recruit-screening methods?

a. criminal record check
b. polygraph exam
c. physical agility test
d. written aptitude test

30. Which of the following represents a successful PCR (police-community relations) program implemented in many municipalities?

a. neighborhood watch
b. speed trap
c. riot control
d. cash for guns programs

31. Which of the following actions is the primary responsibility of a first responder at a crime scene?

a. begin investigation
b. secure the crime scene
c. take photographs
d. compile a report

32. Which of the following describes the current era of policing?

a. Political Era
b. Reform Era
c. Community Era
d. Homeland Security Era

33. Which of the following criminal offenses would be considered a felony?

a. petty theft
b. one punishable by fine and supervised probation
c. one punishable by a year or more in prison
d. one punishable by community service

34. Which of the following defenses to a prosecution would be considered a "procedural defense"?

a. insanity
b. police fraud
c. self-defense
d. alibi

35. Which of the following describes integrity as it appears in the Law Enforcement Oath of Honor?

a. breaking face with the public trust
b. the jurisdiction and citizens served
c. the qualities that distinguish an individual
d. being the same person in both private and public life

36. Which of the following is forbidden by FBI deadly force policy?

a. shooting at a fleeing suspect
b. giving verbal warnings
c. firing at vehicles
d. firing warning shots

37. What aspect of intelligence gathering does NOT justify a police officer's search?

a. the use of inherent coercion
b. the use of anonymous informants
c. the use of criminal informants
d. the use of interrogation

38. Which of the following actions would be considered "role malfeasance" as it applies to police corruption?

a. sale of confiscated drugs
b. destruction of evidence
c. racial profiling
d. non-justifiable homicide

39. What do you call a petty crime that demoralizes the community?

a. recidivism
b. capital offense
c. quality-of-life offense
d. community offense

40. Which of the following terms means that law enforcement officers exercise choice in their application of authority?

a. police discretion
b. police brutality
c. forensics
d. community policing

41. What is the underlying assumption at the core of problem-solving policing?

a. Crime prevention is measured by the number of arrests.
b. Crime statistics can help officers direct patrols.
c. Crime has a contagious effect on young minds.
d. Crime is caused by inherent social inequities.

42. How many female chiefs of police are there in the United States?

a. less than ten
b. around fifty
c. more than one hundred
d. more than five hundred

43. Which group increased their presence on US police forces the most during the 1990s?

a. African-American officers
b. white officers
c. Hispanic officers
d. Asian-American officers

44. Which of the pairs of actions below are known as *Miranda* triggers, meaning both actions are required before the suspect needs to be read *Miranda* warnings?

a. arrest and indictment
b. indictment and bail haring
c. interrogation and arrest
d. arrest and handcuffing

45. The case of *Mapp* v. *Ohio* was important to law enforcement agencies because it made which kind of evidence inadmissible in court?

a. evidence obtained from an illegal search
b. evidence obtained from hearsay
c. evidence obtained under duress
d. evidence obtained from an undercover officer

46. The right of defendants to be confronted by witnesses against them is given in which of the following amendments of the United States Constitution?

a. Fourth
b. Fifth
c. Sixth
d. Seventh

47. In the case of *Escobedo* v. *Illinois*, the court found that the police denied Daniel Escobedo which of his rights?

a. the right to privacy
b. the right to confront witnesses
c. the right to a speedy trial
d. the right to counsel

48. What is the exclusionary rule?

a. Illegally obtained evidence must be excluded from trial.
b. Perjured testimony must be excluded from trial.
c. Confessions made without counsel must be excluded from trial.
d. DNA evidence must be excluded from trial.

49. Which of the following rights does the Fifth Amendment guarantee?

a. no warrants without probable cause
b. no excessive punishment
c. no double jeopardy
d. right to trial by jury

50. Which of the following would be considered a suspicionless search permitted by the Supreme Court?

a. a search of a home that a fugitive was seen running into
b. a mandatory drug test of railway crews
c. a search of the clothing of a suspect fleeing from police
d. a mandatory search of students' lockers in a high school